"Gird your loins, put on the breastplate, and take up the sword. That's the effect this book has. It is not for the faint of heart or those who are intimidated by this culture. It is written for those who are deadly serious about reaching and keeping this digital generation. Statistics record they have become an unreached people group, 'a tribe apart' with their own language, values, customs, and dress. How else can we explain the explosion of youth ministries in history while witnessing an implosion of youth won."

—DR. JAY STRACK
President, StudentLeadership.net

"Those who have been struck by lightning say that right before it hits, you feel a tingle and your hair stands up. That is how I am feeling as a youth leader and youth professor these days. Sovereign God can and will do exactly as He pleases, but my hunch is that He is about to raise up young people to lead the church and then the culture into revival. That is why it is essential that clear voices, such as Alvin Reid's, call the church to raise the bar in student ministry. I disagree with those who say youth ministry is a failed model and that baby and bath both should be thrown out. Alvin Reid has it right—let's minister to students in an atmosphere that recognizes their potential, calls them to God's highest standards, and gives them clear ways to join God in changing the world."

—DR. RICHARD ROSS
Spokesperson, True Love Waits
Professor of Youth and Student Ministry
Southwestern Baptist Theological Seminary

"Alvin Reid is who you want on speed-dial if you need to know anything about people in today's culture and how to respond to them with the gospel. He knows his stuff! My favorite chapter is the 'Advice to Parents.' This is a great resource I'll definitely want on my bookshelf."

—CAROLYN CURTIS
Editor, *On Mission* magazine
North American Mission Board, SBC

"In *Raising the Bar*, Alvin Reid cuts against the grain of the pop youth ministry fun-and-games approach. He calls youth leaders to call students to action, commitment, and full surrender to the King of Kings and cause of causes. This book will inspire and infuriate. It will inspire youth leaders and infuriate the devil!"

—GREG STIER
President, Dare 2 Share Ministries

"Recognizing we are in a new millennium, *Raising the Bar* is a fresh look at youth and culture that challenges us to denote the past, define the present, and determine the future of our youth ministries."

—DR. S. L. SHERRILL
Superintendent, North Raleigh Christian Academy

raising the bar

raising the bar

Ministry to Youth
in the New Millennium

alvin l. reid

Kregel
Academic & Professional

Raising the Bar: Ministry to Youth in the New Millennium

© 2004 by Alvin L. Reid

Published by Kregel Publications, P.O. Box 2607, Grand Rapids, MI 49501.

Cover design: John M. Lucas

Library of Congress Cataloging-in-Publication Data
Reid, Alvin L.
    Raising the bar: ministry to youth in the new millennium / by Alvin L. Reid
        p. cm.
Includes bibliographical references.
    1. Church work with teenagers. I. Title.
BV4447.R42   2004
259'.23—dc22   2004001329

ISBN   0-8254-3632-x

Printed in the United States of America

05 06 07 08 09 / 6 5 4 3

To my wife, Michelle.
I can now say I have been married
a little over half my life—
the best half for sure. Thank you, honey,
for walking with me on this
incredible journey of
parenting and ministry.
The best is yet to come.

Contents

Foreword

Over the past generation, American culture has changed at a meteoric rate. Young people stand at the front edge of that change, in many ways ahead of older adults—such as in their technological savvy and flexibility. But today's youth also stand at a critical crossroads in history: floating in a sea of relativism, of nonlinear thinking, of broken homes and shattered dreams, and weary of anything phony, this generation cries out for significance.

Inside the church, well-meaning youth pastors and youth ministries have developed, sometimes with the unintentional consequences of separating families; encouraging adolescent rather than mature behavior; and—perhaps most significantly—failing to challenge teens, who are at their greatest-ever potential for learning. It seems obvious that over the past generation we have failed to see a movement of students ready to step into the world as a force for Christ. Against this backdrop, Alvin Reid challenges the church to raise the bar.

Perhaps never before have youth been so ready for, and in need of, genuine biblical truth, deep and meaningful relationships, and the kind of real, in-your-face Christianity that characterized the first-century church. One of the encouraging signs of this generation of teens is their desire to be challenged. And who better than the church to challenge students to make a great impact with their lives? *Raising the Bar* offers practical advice for parents, youth workers, pastors, and youth pastors. It challenges the status quo of youth ministry with effective ways to set a new standard for the Millennial Generation.

Reid demonstrates how God has used youth in movements that changed history, from the Great Awakenings to the Jesus Movement. He argues that those called adolescents in contemporary culture are often regarded as heroes in Scripture—Joseph, David, Josiah, Mary, to name a few. And he states that students who learn geometry and trigonometry in high school can learn theology at church! More than anything, he calls church leaders to see teens, not only as a group of people in need of ministry, but as the very ones who could lead a charge for radical obedience that would have a great impact on our culture.

If you are content with the current status of ministry to students, don't read this book! But if you believe that the same nation that produced a LeBron James, who became a star in the NBA at age eighteen, or a Cassie Bernall, a teenaged martyr for Christ, can also produce a generation of teens capable of rising to a new standard rather than settling for whatever is out there, this book is for you. We can wring our hands in despair at the future ahead of our youth or we can see this time as a great opportunity to change the status quo and set a new course. Reid challenges us to do the latter, and for the glory of God, we must!

JOSH MCDOWELL
Dallas, Texas

Acknowledgments

Many people have assisted me in my thinking. While many must be thanked, only I am responsible for any shortfalls the book may have. Countless hours have been spent bouncing ideas off people like Voddie Baucham; Jeff Pratt of InQuest Ministries; Vince Pienski, the youth pastor at our church; and many others. My students at Southeastern and hundreds of churches where I've ministered have provided a two-tiered laboratory for me to think through the ideas you will read about in *Raising the Bar*. Ken Coley, my colleague who knows both the inside and outside of youth ministry, has challenged me to think hard at times about things I have to say. My colleague, New Testament scholar David Alan Black, with his book *The Myth of Adolescence,* paved the way for someone like me, who ministers mainly outside the youth ministry subculture, to challenge the status quo. Others, including Richard Ross at Southwestern Baptist Theological Seminary, student pastor and InQuest Ministries cofounder Steve Wright, and many others I have failed to mention, have helped beyond measure.

The students at Southeastern Baptist Theological Seminary are the best on the planet. They helped me see the opportunity before us if we raise the bar. In particular the team who travels with me in ministry, including the band Joy Made Full, helped not only to shape these concepts, but to shape me as well. Thanks to Lori Calloway, Trent Eayrs, April Johnson, Jenny Justice, Christina Middleton, Bryan Pickering, and Matt Lytle. In addition, Tommy Kiker, suffering through a Ph.D. with me, helped greatly with research.

Southeastern Seminary granted me a sabbatical leave to research this subject, for which I am grateful. I give a special thanks to evangelist Bailey Smith, who has been not only a faithful evangelist for a long time, but he and his precious wife, Sandy, raised three outstanding sons who demonstrate much of what I say in *Raising the Bar*. Bailey raised the funds for the chair I occupy at Southeastern, so without him I wouldn't be there. Thanks, Bailey. My president, Paige Patterson, has been incredibly encouraging in this endeavor. A series of doctoral seminars taught at Southern Baptist Theological Seminary began the sabbatical and set up a wonderful spring of research and thought. Thanks also to Denise Quinn, my faithful and skilled secretary; and to Alana Adams and Marva Bailey, who helped to type the manuscript.

Over the years I've bounced my ideas off literally thousands of adults, young and old. All the e-mails, instant messages, letters, and personal comments from students have blessed my socks off. The youth of Faith Baptist Church, Youngsville, North Carolina, have become some of the most precious people on earth to me. Thanks for putting up with "Brotha Alvin" so much, gang!

Finally, I thank God, whom I serve, for my family. They raise the bar when it comes to standards. Josh—my teen son who amazes me and my wife, Michelle, with his conviction for Christ—and Hannah—who, more than anyone we know, loves people—are blessings beyond description.

Every Generation
Must Be Taught Anew

Larry Gene Ashbrook entered the Wedgwood Baptist Church in Fort Worth, Texas, carrying two pistols. It was the evening of September 15, 1999, a date that has been chiseled into the collective memory of the nation as have only a few other fateful dates. December 7, 1941, and Pearl Harbor is etched on the minds of my parents' generation. November 23, 1963, and the assassination of President John F. Kennedy will be forever etched in the minds of my generation. September 11, 2001, and terrorist attacks on the World Trade Center and the Pentagon will remain etched on the minds of the Buster generation.

But the events of September 15, 1999, say much about the coming generation. That day, just a few months after the tragedy at Columbine, I'd taught class as usual, challenging my students to live radically for Jesus. I asked them a couple of rhetorical questions: "What will it take for the church to awaken in America? Will it take armed gunmen entering our churches, guns blazing?"

That very evening, Larry Ashbrook, age forty-six, launched his assault at Wedgwood. Years earlier, my wife, Michelle, had been a secretary at that church while I attended seminary, and we'd been active members. Now we watched the news in horror, hearing how this man killed seven people at a "See You at the Pole" youth rally.

That evening illustrates what I present in *Raising the Bar*. I believe that God is drawing a line in the sand for the church, and that it's being drawn for this coming generation. It's time to awaken. It's time to get real. It's time to jettison our recreational Christianity for the radical New Testament kind.

How, though, does the shooting at Wedgwood Baptist relate to the coming generation and that line in the sand?

As Ashbrook moved through the church that night, he fired almost 100 rounds of ammunition. A young man named Jeremiah, who had only recently gotten serious about his walk with God, sat in a pew, praying.

Ashbrook shouted, "Your religion [expletive]!"

Jeremiah Neitz could not keep silent. "No, sir, it doesn't," he said as he turned to face the gunman.

"Yes it does!" cried a more irritated Ashbrook.

"No, sir, it doesn't."

Neitz then stood, facing Ashbrook, who was hardly a pew's-length away. "What you need is Jesus Christ," Neitz said. Ashbrook fired more shots—but not at Neitz. The youth's words seemed to confuse the gunman. He slumped into a pew at the rear of the sanctuary, with what witnesses described as a look of disbelief on his face. As he sat, Neitz stood.

Ashbrook aimed the gun at Jeremiah's head. "Sir," Neitz said, "you can shoot me if you want. I know where I'm going—I'm going to heaven." A shot was fired—but not at Neitz. Ashbrook had put the gun to his own head, ending his life.

One person, a youth only recently returning to God, stopped the killing. A young man passionate for Jesus stood courageously for his Master.[1]

Lana Bull, a Southwestern Baptist Seminary student at the rally, said the last statement of the gunman before his death was, "I'm not interested in y'all. I wanted *adults*."[2]

Yet it took a very *adult* act for Jeremiah Neitz to stand up to a gunman and share Christ. Young people can and do make mature, responsible decisions. But contemporary culture, even within the church, has developed a mistaken mind-set: Youth are kids who need to be baby-sat, rather than young adults ready for the challenge of changing the world.

The teen years, or the years primarily targeted by youth ministry, are in many ways the most important years of a person's life. More seeds of ministry are sown in youth between the ages of twelve and eighteen, more relationships forged that affect their future, more choices made with long-term implications, than arguably any other period in life. These are the years when young adults begin to think about issues that will influence the rest of their lives.

So how are we doing in preparing them? *Raising the Bar* doesn't indict contemporary youth ministry. Rather, part 1 discusses how the evangelical church is doing in preparing youth, or students, or young adults (*Raising the Bar* uses all three terms synonymously) to face the adult world. And more than that, how are we doing in preparing them to cross that line in the sand? *Raising the Bar* doesn't present a surefire formula for creating the ideal youth ministry of the twenty-first century. Rather, part 2 suggests areas in which the potential of youth may be unleashed.

Young people are not children finishing childhood; they're young adults preparing for adulthood, and they will rise to the bar we set for them. We can give them encouragement through a word of praise, a pat on the back, or a hug. But sometimes the best encouragement is a kick in the pants.

As I tell my students, it's the job of a minister both to comfort the afflicted *and* to afflict the comfortable. Whether you're a pastor, youth pastor, youth worker, parent, or any combination thereof, may the words that follow challenge you to get out of your comfort zone when it comes to working with youth, encourage you about the quality of today's young people, and help you evaluate your view of today's youth.

This new generation is poised to make a difference—to *change* their world to the glory of God. May we draw a line in the sand and raise the bar.

And let's start *today.*

PART 1

Test Time: Does Youth Ministry Pass?

Imagine Jesus taking His disciples up to a mountain. He gathers them around, and teaches them for a while, saying, "Blessed are the poor in spirit, for theirs is the kingdom of heaven. Blessed are the meek. Blessed are they that mourn. Blessed are the merciful. Blessed are they that search for justice."

Then Simon Peter asks, "Do we have to write this down?"

And Andrew asks, "Will this be on the test?"

And Philip says, "I don't have a pencil."

And James asks, "Do we have to turn this in?"

And John says, "That's not fair, the other disciples didn't have to learn this."

And Judas asks, "What does this have to do with real life?"

Then one of the religious authorities standing nearby says, "Where is your lesson plan and the teaching outline of your major points? Where is your anticipatory set and learning objectives in the cognitive domain?"

And Jesus wept.

In a perfect world, students would never have to take exams or quizzes. Professors would never have to grade tests or papers. Because students would be so motivated to learn, they'd devour their assignments and only miss class for an appendectomy or a concussion.

But this is not a perfect world. We need to conduct tests to insure that students are ready to meet the challenges of adult life. Suppose, for example, a member of your church has a brain tumor. The young surgeon tells you prior to the surgery, "I've read the books, watched some operations, and have complete confidence in my ability . . . but no one's ever tested me to see if I can, in fact, successfully perform the surgery." Would you want that young surgeon to operate on your sick member?

Suppose, now, that your dear Uncle Joe is unsaved and that you've been praying for him for twenty years. A young person says to you, "I've attended youth meetings since grade school, and I've participated in the usual church activities for youth." Would you want that young person to witness to your Uncle Joe?

Ministry deals with eternity—a matter more vital than even brain surgery. You may or may not agree with much of what *Raising the Bar* says about youth ministry. But consider—in a secular world, students are tested both academically and physically. Does it not make sense for youth in our churches to pass the spiritual test and be ready to enter a fallen world as capable adults?

> Youth in church are underchallenged and treated as children. We can raise the bar to produce biblical champions.

If we conducted spiritual tests on students in our churches, tests with a standard comparable to a physical fitness test or an academic exam such as the SAT, the vast majority would probably fail miserably. And the fault would not lie with them. Many parents complain about low academic standards in some of our public schools. But has the church considered what kind of standard we're setting in preparing a generation of young adults?

I issue this challenge. We can raise the bar for this generation. But we can't do it unless we admit that the bar has been set too low, for too long. And this challenge to youth ministry is as much for me as for you. I have a teenage son, and my daughter will hit those years sooner than I care to admit. So the very words that I write apply to my teaching as well.

It's time to raise the bar.

Chapter One

Meet the Millennials
The Next Great Generation

> *Then the king instructed Ashpenaz, the master of his eunuchs, to bring some of the children of Israel and some of the king's descendants and some of the nobles, young men in whom there was no blemish, but good-looking, gifted in all wisdom, possessing knowledge and quick to understand, who had ability to serve in the king's palace, and whom they might teach the language and literature of the Chaldeans. . . .*
>
> *But Daniel purposed in his heart that he would not defile himself with the portion of the king's delicacies, nor with the wine which he drank; therefore he requested of the chief of the eunuchs that he might not defile himself.*
>
> —Daniel 1:3–4, 8

P.S. Honestly, I want to live completely for God. It's hard and scary, but totally worth it." Cassie Bernall handed this note to her friend Amanda at Columbine High School the morning of the day she died.[1]

Cassie didn't make it to graduation. Before joining the class of 2000, she answered *yes* when a young gunman asked if she was a Christian—and Cassie died as a martyr. But her zeal for God and desire to make an impact illustrates the smoldering potential of the coming, great generation.

The idea for the title of this chapter comes from Neil Howe and William Strauss, *Millennials Rising: The Next Great Generation* (New York: Vintage, 2000).

23

A Line in the Sand

Martyrdom in America was once about as likely as glaciers in the Sahara; now it's become a reality. In our day, we're witnessing for the first time in our history the martyrdom of significant numbers on American soil. And the martyrs are young people. At Columbine, some students were singled out for their faith. At Wedgwood Baptist Church, students died for simply gathering to worship.

Yet these youth represent a generation who, while observing a zealous conviction in those outside the church, see few adults within the church offering students a challenge. Young people in our churches see, for instance, youthful militants in the Middle East who, in the name of faith, are raised up with the hope of being suicide bombers. To what, in the name of faith, do we raise our youth to aspire? Perhaps it's time to challenge our youth to a higher standard of conviction within the church.

Maybe God is drawing a line in the sand today. It wouldn't be the first time. He drew one for Noah's generation, and that patriarch was challenged to an incredible act of faith and to regenerate humanity from a single family. In the book of Numbers, after guiding a generation through the wilderness for forty years, God drew a line just outside the Promised Land. That generation failed in their belief, and failed to cross the line into their inheritance. In the sixth century B.C., God drew a line in the sand, and it stopped generations of Israelites from enjoying their own nation. They were taken into captivity at the hand of the Babylonians.

But there He provided a new generation of leaders to start afresh in that foreign land. He started with youth: Daniel, Shadrach, Meshach, and Abednego set the standard for the Jews in Babylon.

These young Hebrews had every reason to cave in to their culture. They were, after all, only young people. Certainly they were among the best and brightest. But they were still young—probably middle-school aged. Many scholars set their ages at thirteen to fifteen. Some say they could have been only twelve. But when asked to eat food that might compromise their faith (merely eat food, mind you—not defile themselves with prostitutes), they refused. Later, as older men, they would face everything from a fiery furnace to a den of lions. And no matter what the odds, they stood for God.

These men demonstrate that the most important years are the early ones. If young people have not formed convictions by then, they will likely never form any. It is during these impressionable years that most people determine *how* they will decide upon the most important matters in their future. That's why youth can and should be challenged to surrender to the lordship of Jesus.

At the same time they must be reminded of what that surrender entails. Involving Christ in the decisions they make about dating and how they view material possessions will affect their decisions about whom they will marry and the careers they choose. True, many elements in the lives of young adults are still in flux—one survey said 53 percent of college graduates follow careers outside their major—but the seeds that are sown today in young people will continue to sprout for the rest of their lives. Will the fruit that is produced sustain another Noah, or a Daniel—or Cassie Bernall?

Today's New Generation

In order to minister effectively to today's youth, we have to understand a few things about them. And the graduating high school class of 2000 has been more studied, interviewed, and analyzed than any other in American history. I, too, have ample opportunity to observe and interact with today's youth, spending much of my time in churches, at camps, and in conferences, speaking annually to thousands of teens. Below are a few observations I've garnered about the cultural environment in which the Millennials were born:

1. They have no meaningful recollection of the Reagan era and do not know the president was shot.
2. They don't remember the Cold War.
3. They're too young to remember Tiananmen Square.
4. Their lifetime has always included AIDS.
5. The expression "you sound like a broken record" means nothing to them, because vinyl records predate them.
6. They've always had an answering machine and a DVD player.
7. They cannot fathom not having a remote control.

8. The Vietnam War is as ancient to them as World War I, World War II, or even the Civil War.
9. They have no idea that Americans were ever held hostage in Iran.
10. They've never heard the phrases "Where's the beef?" "I'd walk a mile for a Camel," or "de plane, de plane!"
11. They don't care who shot J.R. because they have no idea who J.R. is.
12. There's always been MTV.

Their Cultural Center

The above list offers a cultural orientation of today's students, but of importance, too, are events that influence this new generation. For graduating high school seniors in the year 2000, the most influential event was Columbine. That is, until September 11, 2001. Never before has any American generation seen a level of terrorism to equal the attacks on the World Trade Center and the Pentagon.

Yet these explosive events, although worthy of significant attention, can cause us to the miss less noticeable yet more critical long-term trends that impact American youth. By focusing on the traumatic and immediate events that capture the headlines, might we miss the larger, deeper shifts in the cultural center?

One of these shifts in the cultural center relates to generation. Some observers place too much emphasis on generational differences, but we're wise to note the climate, or the season, in which we live. And there *are* definite differences in the cultural center of each generation.

While no clear mark delineates a generational era, recent generations are typically arranged accordingly:

- **Builders:** Born 1927–1945
- **Boomers:** Born 1946–1964
- **Busters:** Born 1965–1981
- **Millennials:** Born 1982–2002

The generation beginning with those born about 1981–1982 is called Generation Y, the Net-Gens, Millennials, Mosaics (Barna), Echoboomers, and Bridgers. Barna dates the Millennials from 1984, whereas I follow

Howe and Strauss, beginning at 1982. I chose the term *Millennial* for two reasons. First, I didn't want to come up with yet another term (there are already enough). Second, when surveyed as to what they would like to be called, the older members of this generation chose the term *Millennial.*

For my generation, the Boomer culture was marked by borderline self-worship and could be described in the phrase "get ahead." The Buster culture could be described by the phrase "get lost." But the Millennial culture could be described by the phrase "get real."

Defining generations, though, is far from an exact science. I issue two cautions: first, every person of any culture and any generation has many things in common with other humans. Physically, spiritually, and emotionally, the similarities across the centuries are striking. All are created in the image of God, all have sinned, all need a Savior whose name is Jesus, all have the ultimate destiny of heaven or hell. So in the macroscopic view of things, generational differences—although they do matter—can easily be overemphasized.

Second, this postmodern world—in which the Millennials will be the first full-fledged members—bears a similarity, philosophically, to that which the New Testament church faced. The pluralism and relativism of the first century have again become significant forces in culture. In such a climate, the early believers' exclusive claim that Jesus was the only way of salvation was met with hostility, even as in our day a so-called "tolerance" leads many to attack evangelical believers for the gospel we share. The times they are a-changing! In determining how best to deal with this generation, we who work and live with the Millennials would do well, then, to immerse ourselves in the Word.

Their Cultural Shift

That being said, obvious differences exist between generations. And to better understand how critical this generation is to a fallen world, we must compare it to earlier ones in American history.

Barna gives a good summary of the shift from Builders to Baby Boomers:

If there was ever a group that should have understood the need to enter the cultural scene with a major statement, it should have been the Boomers. After all, they had replaced the Builder generation in the '60s with a series of high-profile, in-your-face transitions. Elvis Presley and Chuck Berry, the most radical musical pioneers adored by the last of the Builder teens, were positively angelic in comparison to the wild hair, daring lyrics and ear-shattering rock of the Beatles, Jimmy [sic] Hendrix, The Who, and Led Zeppelin. . . . Woodstock, the cultural coming-out party of the Boomers, was unlike anything the Builders had ever imagined, much less carried out. Rather than accepting conditions as they were, Boomers questioned everything—until they got the answer they wanted.[2]

If the relationship between the Builders and Boomers was the Generation Gap, then Barna rightly refers to the relationship between Boomers and Busters as the Generational Cold War. Researchers indicate, though, a clear shift in the rising generation of young people. And the relationship between Millennials and their parents—younger Boomers and older Busters—will be, I believe, the Generational Gathering, for family is returning as a major part of the lives of this new generation.

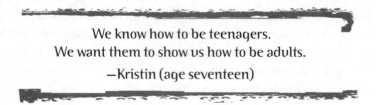

We know how to be teenagers.
We want them to show us how to be adults.
—Kristin (age seventeen)

Those who study generations have observed a subtle truth in the lives of thousands of teens across America. They look to adults—both family members and spiritual leaders—for real guidance. I spoke recently with the minister of students at a strong church in Florida. His comment has been echoed by scores of youth pastors: "Student ministers are realizing that this generation of young people [is] not satisfied with the latest game or icebreaker. They want real, honest, biblical substance." I asked one seventeen-year-old named Kristin, "What advice should I give to those who work with youth?" Kristin said, "Tell them we know how to be teenagers. We want them to show us how to be adults."

These Millennials want us to teach them not only to be adults, they want us to teach them to be godly adults. At a conference a few years ago, Richard Ross—now professor of youth ministry at Southwestern Baptist Theological Seminary, and probably the man who knows more youth pastors than anyone in the nation—made this observation: "Across America I am hearing from student ministers that something is happening among the sixteen and under population. There seems to be a growing desire in the coming generation to honor God." That piqued my interest, as similar testimonies have been repeated to me by many student pastors and youth.

Thus, I am confident about the future. I don't see the world through rose-colored glasses, nor am I a glib optimist who ignores real issues (like youth ministry challenges). But I'm convinced that God is in control of the universe, and that He is living and active in this world.

Daniel of the Old Testament and his three young friends had every reason to collapse—snatched from their home and their homeland while so young, facing the brainwashing Babylonians. But they saw God's work in the midst of that, and so should we.

The wind of the Spirit blows where it will. We do not tell God what to do. But if we journey with Him, we, like good sailors, can set the sails to go with the wind of His Spirit. And a refreshing wind is moving among the youth in our country. God is raising up a new generation. As leaders and parents, we would do well to set the sails in a manner that uplifts this coming generation.

Overrating Youth Rebellion

Youth as a time of rebellion has long been a stereotype. Howe and Strauss succinctly rebut that stereotype in their provocative book *Millennials Rising: The Next Great Generation.*[3] The authors begin with the youth-culture stereotype that is promoted by media:

> Until recently, the public has been accustomed to nonstop media chatter about bad kids. . . . To believe the news, you'd suppose our schools are full of kids who can't read in the classroom,

shoot one another in the hallways, spend their loose change on
tongue rings, and couldn't care less who runs the country.[4]

This sounds like not only the media depiction of youth, it also sounds
like the attitude of parents and others talking about the youth at church.
But Howe and Strauss's view differs, and I think they're right:

> Meet the Millennials, born on or after 1982.
>   As a group, Millennials are unlike any other youth generation
> in living memory. They are more numerous, more affluent, bet-
> ter educated, and more ethnically diverse. More important, they
> are beginning to manifest a wide array of positive social habits
> that older Americans no longer associate with youth, including a
> new focus on teamwork, achievement, modesty, and good con-
> duct. Only a few years from now, this can-do youth revolution
> will overwhelm the cynics and the pessimists. Over the next de-
> cade, the Millennial Generation will entirely recast the image of
> youth from downbeat and alienated to upbeat and engaged—
> with potentially seismic consequences for America.[5]

Virtually every conversation with hundreds of parents, scores of youth
pastors, and thousands of teens in recent years has led me to the conclusion that Howe and Strauss's general assessment of the Millennial generation is accurate. This doesn't mean every student will suddenly become
a follower of Jesus and a perfect child. Many problems face this generation (many not of their own making). The Howard Sterns and the
Eminems of this world profit on shock, performing on the edge of soci-
etal acceptance. So we dare not underestimate the evil that these young
people face. Nor do we dare underestimate their potential for greatness.
We'd do well to avoid constantly noting only what is wrong with youth.
A steady emphasis on youth problems and the evils of youth culture can
be not only a self-fulfilling prophecy—it's just plain wrong.
    The following is a list of the Millennial generation's positive charac-
teristics. Most of them come from the work of Howe and Strauss, but
I've added a few.[6]
    1. They're not pessimists, they're optimists. Contrast this with the more

pessimistic Buster generation who preceded them. In a recent survey, nine in ten Millennials describe themselves as happy, positive, or confident. Every survey that I've seen, in fact, reports the same of this generation.

Barna agrees, noting that the differences in generations are seen in attitude more than anything else. Busters, for example, tend to see the glass as half empty, while Millennials tend to see the glass as half full. They are more upbeat, less cynical. They are more interested in a meaningful career, and view education as vital. Barna found that nine out of ten also revel in their self-sufficiency, so confident are they about the future.[7] His research indicates that it's the adults who are pessimistic, not the youth.

> The first tough, cranky, pragmatic, independent Generation Xers are gonna start hitting 40 in the next couple of years, and rearing up behind them are the Millennials, the first batch of which are the high school class of 2000. These kids are, as a group, pleasant, cheerful, helpful, ambitious, and community-oriented.
>
> —MaryAnn Johanson
> Film critic, flickfilosopher.com[8]

2. They're not self-absorbed, they're cooperative team players. I've personally noticed a remarkable change in youth groups in the past three years, particularly in their commitment to group activities, including evangelistic outreach. This generation has been raised on Barney and the Power Rangers, who focused on working together as a group. This is the generation that's contributing to the phenomenal success of Upward Basketball in churches across the land. They are remarkably committed to missions projects and personal evangelism when sent out in teams.

I recently spoke to almost two thousand Korean students in a rally led by one of my students at Southeastern. Did those students come to the rally to hear me? Not exactly! They came to be participants in a huge basketball tournament. The rally simply kicked off the event.

3. They're not distrustful, they accept authority. One study found that the people to whom twelve- to fourteen-year-olds look most for answers were their parents. Barna notes, "Family is a big deal to teenagers, regardless of how they act or what they say. It is the rare teenager who believes he or she can lead a fulfilling life without receiving complete acceptance and support from his or her family." He adds, "In spite of the seemingly endless negative coverage in the media about the state of the family these days, most teens are proud of their family."[9]

4. They're not rule-breakers, they're rule-followers. From 1995 to 2000, homicide, violent crime, abortion, and pregnancy among teens dropped at a faster rate than during any previous period. In a fascinating critique of Baby Boomers' pessimism concerning the present younger generation, Mike Males is scathing:

> Suburban chronicler Patricia Hersch brands the entire younger generation "an insidious . . . tribe apart." The media's newest youth-violence expert, psychologist James Garbarino, warns the "epidemic . . . of lethal youth violence . . . has spread throughout American society. . . ."
>
> But did the Lord of the Flies ensue? To the contrary. Perhaps no period in history has witnessed such rapid improvements in adolescent conduct. From 1990 through 1999, teenage violence and other malaise plunged: homicide rates (down 62 percent), rape (down 27 percent), violent crime (down 22 percent), school violence (down 20 percent), property offenses (down 33 percent), births (down 17 percent), abortions (down 15 percent), sexually transmitted diseases (down 50 percent), violent deaths (down 20 percent), suicide (down 16 percent), and drunken driving fatalities (down 35 percent).
>
> Unhealthy youth indexes have fallen to three-decade lows while good ones—school graduation, college enrollment, community volunteerism—are up. . . . Overall, 80 percent to 90 percent of today's supposedly "depressed, lonely, alienated, confused" younger generation consistently tells surveyors they're happy, self-confident, and like their parents.[10]

Males' opinion is echoed by Chris Lehmann:

As almost no media outlet is going to tell you, kids these days are astonishingly well-adjusted, nonviolent, educated, and polite. . . . A record number of American teens volunteer their time to charitable causes—twice as many as their counterparts of 20 years past. Math SATs are at a 30-year high, even teen literacy is increasing: A recent survey conducted by the National Education Association found that 41 percent of teen respondents said they read 15 books or more a year. How many adults can claim a comparable intake? [11]

Lehmann concludes with this surprising statistical evidence:

16 school-age victims were killed in violent crime incidents . . . on or near schools over the 2000–2001 academic year; 19 violent deaths, including suicides, occurred on or near school grounds the year before. Meanwhile, abusive adults still kill children at the remarkably high rate of five fatalities a day.[12]

Perhaps those of us who work with youth should look in the mirror every time we complain about youth problems.

5. They're not neglected, they're watched over. While broken homes abound like never before, this generation's parents show a greater concern for the well-being of their children than did those parents immediately preceding them. In the summer of 2002, a number of child abductions received unprecedented national attention, not because such crimes are on the rise, but because concern for children nationally is on the rise. From the Amber Alert to a change in the approach of anti-drug public service spots (like the one I saw last week with the caption "Parents: The Anti-Drug"), a stress on parental issues is on the rise. (More about this later.)

6. They're not racist, they're color-blind. If your church could be aptly renamed the "The Church of You Are Not My Kind," say good-bye to youth. In a few years you won't have any. Youth today are militantly color-blind. A 1999 survey on interracial dating found that 82 percent of youth said love is color-blind.[13] My son gets angry at the thought of a church that would exclude someone on the basis of skin color.

7. They're not stupid, they're very bright. This generation understands technology better than their parents. For example, my daughter, a younger Millenial, was quite adept at CD-Rom technology at age four. In fact she was better at it than I was, so I grounded her. Okay, not really.

Journalist Michael Lewis notes youth who are affecting such normally *verboten* realms as Wall Street. He describes "Marcus Arnold, the fifteen-year-old who dispenses legal advice on the Internet to eager adults; [and] Johnathan Lebed, another fifteen-year-old who roils the Securities and Exchange Commission with his stock recommendations, and buys a $41,000 Mercedes with some of the $800,000 he makes trading stocks on the Net—a car he's too young to drive."[14]

8. They have not given up on progress, they believe in the future. The idealism of the '60s generation is seen in the Millennials, but without so much of the anti-authority edge. Volunteerism among youth has soared over the past few years. A pastor told me recently that 50 to 60 percent of the teens he talks with say "they are very desirous of making a difference in the world."

9. They're not unmotivated, they simply want to be challenged. We decry low academic standards in public schools, claiming that they teach to the lowest common denominator and are unaware that the majority of their students are capable of rising to an academic challenge. Yet in our churches, we are guilty of the same low standards. Youth today are inventing computer games, playing in the NBA, winning gold in the Olympics, and dying as martyrs. Churches must increase the level of expectations that we have for them. If they can learn chemistry in high school, they can learn theology at church.

Johnny Hunt is pastor of one of the greatest churches in America, the First Baptist Church of Woodstock, Georgia. Few churches in the nation reach more youth in a year than does First Baptist. While flying with me to a conference in 2002, Pastor Hunt told me that 180 youth met at his church every Sunday morning at 7:15 A.M. to sing in the youth choir and play in the youth orchestra. He recently began challenging students to dedicate a year to mission work following high school. The fall of 2002, seventeen students from First Baptist went to Argentina to spend a year in mission service. Why? Because they were challenged. Barna concurs: "In their ruminations about meaning, purpose and direction, one of the encouraging results is that 9 out of 10 youths believe that it is still possible for one person to make a significant difference in the world. The issue they wrestle with is exactly how to do it."[15]

10. They're not irreligious, they seek genuine spirituality. "Two out of three teens are interested in a meaningful relationship with God," Barna found. "Yet one-third fewer are geared to being active in a church. This is indeed reflective of the youth population's impressions of the local church: It sometimes has something to offer, but what it adds is neither consistent nor important enough to justify a significant commitment to such an entity. If they are going to find God, they believe they can find Him elsewhere."[16]

Barna articulates a great indictment on the state of the youth ministry today. It's obvious that youth ministry in America has not produced a generation of young people who are passionate about the church.

But Barna's finding are also an indictment on the state of the church in America. Howe and Strauss offer a remarkably optimistic view of the coming generation as a whole, but the possibilities for churched youth is even greater. The Census Bureau notes that beginning in the year 2006, the total population of teens will be the greatest in American history.[17] This fact alone should cause leaders in the church to assess their focus on the student population in their churches. The November 2001 *Emerging Trends* newsletter of the Princeton Religion Research Center featured the following headline: "'Millennials' Have Special Role in New, Post-September 11, World." The Princeton Center findings are remarkably similar to those of Howe and Strauss (as well as mine) above.

If Howe and Strauss are correct, why have so few reached the same conclusions? Because "the predictive assumption is wrong," they argue. "Americans habitually assume that the future will be a straight-line extension of the recent past."[18]

What if Howe and Strauss, the Princeton Center, and I are wrong? What if this generation turns out to be the most evil, scary, pathetic generation in history? As believers, we *still* should look through the eyes of faith; imagine how God, through the power of the gospel, could use such a group.

But what if our conclusions are right? What if God is stirring? What if the largest number of youth in history—youth who are optimistic, bright, motivated, spiritual—are unleashed on the American scene? Could we have a movement like the Student Volunteer Movement at the end of the nineteenth century, when thousands of students went to the mission field? What if God purposes to use this generation as catalyst for a great revival?

Ponder this: Do you see through the eyes of faith? Do you perceive the youth whom you know as having the potential for greatness, or do you think of them in terms of the youth problems so often reported today? Have you observed any signs that the Millennials might indeed be rising to make a positive impact? In *Good to Great,* a secular book for the business world, Jim Collins says this: "Good is the enemy of great. . . . We don't have great schools, principally because we have good schools. We don't have great government principally because we have good government. Few people attain great lives, in large part because it is just so easy to settle for a good life."[19]

Collins' words apply to youth ministry as well. "Good" youth ministries abound. Could that be why there are so few young adults accomplishing great things for God?

Chapter Two

Time to Climatize

Analyzing Youth Culture

And do this, knowing the time, that now it is high time to awake out of sleep; for now our salvation is nearer than when we first believed. The night is far spent, the day is at hand. Therefore let us cast off the works of darkness, and let us put on the armor of light. Let us walk properly, as in the day, not in revelry and drunkenness, not in lewdness and lust, not in strife and envy.

—Romans 13:11–13

In February 2003, the unthinkable happened. Jesica Santillan was wheeled into an operating room at one of the most prestigious hospitals in the world. She'd been sick from infancy, but Jesica and her family believed that the complicated operation, involving a rare heart-lung transplant, would give her weakened body new life.

The transplant seemed to go well, then the horrible mistake was discovered. The transplanted heart and lungs were of the wrong blood type. Days later, and following a second attempt at a transplant, Jesica died. Right hospital, right doctors, right procedure, but a wrong match spelled disaster.

Something has gone wrong, too, in the hospitals and operating rooms for the soul. Across America today, many gifted, committed youth ministers and workers, as well as pastors and parents by the thousands, long to see youth thrive. This current generation of youth has more potential for revival, for renewal, for change, than has any in a long time. But a problem faces the church—the youth-ministry approaches we've been using are the wrong match. They have simply failed to develop the potential of youth. We cannot say that, over the past two decades or so, we've raised up a generation of students who have changed the world for Christ.

Years ago I sat in a meeting with church leaders from across the nation. They had convened to discuss evangelizing America, and a leader in evangelizing young people shared with me a statistic that shook me: Over the preceding twenty years the number of full-time youth pastors had grown dramatically, and a plethora of magazines, music, and ideas aimed at youth had been birthed along the way. Meanwhile, during that same time span, the numbers of young people won to Christ *dropped* at about as fast a rate.

"Let me get this straight," I said. "The largest rise of full-time youth ministers in history has been accompanied by the biggest decline in youth evangelism effectiveness?"

"Yes, that is what I am saying," he replied somberly.

> Since the 1970s youth baptisms in the Southern Baptist Convention have been declining. Total youth baptisms reported in 1997 were 93,593. Only fifty SBC churches averaged more than fifty youth baptisms in the last ten years. Of the 38,000 churches reporting that year, 17,500 reported no baptisms in the twelve to seventeen age category; 23,500 churches baptized no more than one. And yet the number of youth ministers has grown.[1]

Today, about a decade after that conversation, the situation hasn't changed a great deal. For the past three decades, then, youth ministry has exploded across America, accompanied by a rise in the number of degrees in youth ministry granted by colleges and seminaries, an abundance of books and other resources, and a network of cottage industries devoted solely to youth ministry. Yet those same three decades have failed to produce a generation of young people who graduate from high school or leave youth groups ready to change the world for Christ.

Now, before you form a lynch squad of youth pastors to come after me, let me say very quickly that I don't think that the rise of youth ministers and the accompanying decline of youth evangelism is necessarily a cause-and-effect relationship. But the failure of contemporary youth ministry to make a positive impact on youth culture cannot be ignored. Thus, *if we keep doing what we're doing, we'll keep getting what we're getting!*

It is not the purpose of *Raising the Bar* to articulate a list of everything that's wrong with contemporary youth ministry. But my research and experience reveals a common denominator: churches across America treat teenagers like fourth graders, and ministry to youth is like a YMCA/YWCA meeting. But as youth ministers and parents, we can set a new standard. We can trade in the latest "bag of tricks" approach for a "raise the-bar-to-change-culture" attitude.

The Power of God

Have you ever lived in a town where half the residents became radical, fanatical followers of Jesus in a couple of years? Have you lived in a neighborhood where instead of sports, clothes, or cars, the subject of conversation for almost everyone was Jesus?

That was the kind of world in which Jonathan Edwards found himself about 250 years ago. In the eighteenth century, God shook the American colonies in a revival movement known as the First Great Awakening. Edwards wrote a treatise entitled *Some Thoughts Concerning the Present Revival of Religion in New England* to describe and defend the movement. This young pastor noticed something most ministers have failed to recognize since: when God begins a new movement of His Spirit, He often uses young people at the heart of it. Note Edwards' comment about the great revival he observed:

> The work has been chiefly amongst the young; and comparatively but few others have been made partakers of it. And indeed it has commonly been so, when God has begun any great work for the revival of his church; he has taken the young people, and has cast off the old and stiff-necked generation.[2]

When I taught at a university, another professor joked one day that teaching would be fun if it weren't for the students. I never quite got the humor in that, because I love students. Today, youth pastors across America could make a similar statement—but with a twist: *youth ministry would be great if it weren't for the "ministry."* On the one hand, youth leaders today have incredible love for young people and a passion to see them grow in Christ. On the other hand, they often report being worn out from ministry. Greg Stier summarizes what I hear almost weekly from youth pastors:

> Maybe it's the complaints about the stains in the carpets or the holes in the walls in the youth room. Perhaps it's the struggle of the juggle—the constant juggling act between parental and pastoral expectations. As a result of those difficulties and a thousand others, many youth leaders eventually give in or give up. They give in to the counter-biblical challenge to reel in their students' exuberance instead of harnessing it and focusing it. They give up on going for the optimum, on stirring the pot, and on swinging for the fences. . . . The result is that youth leaders often slowly transform their roles from passionate visionary to skilled event-coordinator, from mission-driven general to sanctified baby-sitter.[3]

Many youth ministers are simply sick and tired of being sick and tired. As a professor who enjoys critical analysis, playing the devil's advocate, and the opportunity to evaluate movements or theories, I'm increasingly unimpressed with some of the attitudes and approaches used in youth ministry today.

Don't get me wrong—I see much good in many youth ministries, and I love youth pastors. I teach some of the finest people studying for youth ministry on the earth. But one thing is clear: most youth pastors learn youth ministry from other youth pastors who learned youth ministry from youth pastors. Such inbreeding does not encourage serious reflection on ministry practices. Add to that the rapid growth of youth ministry as a separate discipline in the modern church, and little wonder that neither the opportunity nor the time has been afforded for the church as a whole, or for youth ministers for that matter, to critically analyze this field.

I, and a multitude of youth ministers with whom I've spoken, believe it's time to assess the state of youth ministry. An honest, straightforward critique of basic presuppositions and attitudes is needed, as well as an evaluation of the impact that the many cottage industries in the youth field, the various parachurch organizations, and the thousands of youth ministries in churches across America are making in the real world where youth live.

In a nutshell, we must evaluate how the church relates the truth of Christianity to culture. In Romans 13:11, Paul challenges us to be aware of our culture. His saying, "And now, *knowing the time*," does not refer to looking at our watches. The Greek term he uses refers to an intimate, personal knowledge of the season, or the climate, in which we live. In other words, as we preachers of the Word must be able to exegete the Scripture, so must a leader in the church be able to analyze culture.

Contemporary popular culture treats youth as children, not as young adults. Popular culture—from MTV to movies to video games—thrives on maintaining a distinct youth culture for marketing purposes. In the church, our attitudes are not much better. Christian publications and church or parachurch youth ministries deal with the particular, most pressing needs of the times—how to say no to sex, dealing with peer pressure, and so on.

All of these and many more issues are certainly vital, but none of them addresses our basic philosophical approach to young people. The burning question confronting the church today should be less about how young ladies should dress, and more about how we *see* them. Do we see young people as children finishing childhood, and thus in need of activities to keep them occupied, or as young adults ready to take on the challenges of the complex world they will so quickly face?

God has assembled an army of young adults. He has opened a door before the leaders of the church today through which to see a generation of radicals who are ready to be unleashed on the culture. Yet today, they are the most overlooked army in the church. Consider this. Youth are:

- utilized by cultists (look at the thousands of young people who take an annual Mormon mission, for example), but ignored by the church;
- enlisted by our government in times of war, but too often left on the sidelines of spiritual conflict;
- chosen to represent nations at the highest level of athletic endeavor, but pushed aside into secondary status in the body of the Christ;
- often challenged academically in school while fed spiritual baby food in church;
- poised to live for Christ, but too often told to stay out of the way.

Why focus on youth ministry? *First,* as already noted, over the past three years there has been a shift in the commitment level of this generation of youth.

Second, a historical study of spiritual awakenings has raised the question, Why hasn't more been written on the role of youth in the activity of God (perhaps because old people write church history texts)?

Third, discussions with colleagues and others led to the conclusion that current youth ministry has not been effective. The cottage industries related to youth ministry are, although financially lucrative, spiritually anemic. Thousands of students attend various inspirational events, but those events haven't been effective in taking students from an adolescent mind-set to their focusing on doing great things for God. Youth ministers—including many in my classes as well as scores with whom I have talked over the past few years—indicate a growing dissatisfaction with the present state of youth ministry. Who can blame them, with a church culture that treats teens like fourth graders and youth pastors like baby-sitters?

Fourth, if all politics is local, then everything spiritual is personal. My son, Josh, has entered the ranks of young people, and Hannah will be there soon. I can write and preach and teach and make all sorts of bold declarations, but I have only one chance to raise my children. And across America, millions of Christian parents feel the same way. Focusing on youth ministry, then, not only analyzes a subject, it is the effort of a fellow pilgrim trying to find God's best for his own children and those of other parents.

Evaluation Is a Healthy Thing

Louie Giglio has been a strategic leader in a movement called Passion that has helped many students rethink worship. His thoughts on youth ministry offer a succinct overview of what I have also observed:

> First, we need innovative leaders, those who blaze a trail with fresh creativity and *not just a rehashed imitation of the current culture.* Second, *we must have a belief in our students' capacity to grasp more.* . . . Third, we as leaders must . . . *"show the way" and not just "tell the way."* And fourth, we must have a clear strategy so that at the end of the day we don't just have a pile of extended energy but rather the assurance that we've accomplished the goal.[4] (emphasis added)

The meteoric growth of youth ministry in the church over the past generation calls for analysis, evaluation, and reflection. Why? Note the following excerpt from an article by DeVries:

> Although her family was only nominally involved in the church, Jenny came to our youth group faithfully throughout her teenage years. She went on mission trips and attended Sunday school; she was a regular fixture in our program. We had been successful with Jenny, or so we thought.
>
> Jimmy, on the other hand, never quite connected with our youth ministry. We really worked to get him involved with our youth programs. He had no interest in retreats or mission trips; Sunday school bored him, and youth groups seemed a little on the silly side for his taste. He sometimes attended another church across town. On my little scoreboard of kids we had been effective with, Jimmy was on the "lost" side.
>
> But Jimmy had one thing going for him—every Sunday, he was in worship—with his parents at our church or with his friends at another church. Jimmy didn't need our outrageous and creative youth ministry to lead him to faith maturity.
>
> But for Jenny, our youth ministry was her only Christian

connection. Unlike a real family, the youth group "family" forced her to resign when she was too old to fit the requirements. She now looks back on her youth group experience as . . . a fun, even laughable part of her past, but something that belongs exclusively in the realm of her teenage years.

There is something wrong with the standard of success that prematurely rates a leader's work with Jenny as the example of success and Jimmy's as the example of failure.[5]

More than a few youth pastors tell me that the above story is not a rare one. The following e-mail has become familiar:

After 11 years of youth ministry I say that [DeVries' story] is not an exceptional example. I sit with tears in my eyes as I think of all my Jennys. Their names are different . . . but it hurts all the same. DeVries is so on the money when he says we must tie [our youth] to the family—first, their nuclear family, and then the family of God—in a much more meaningful way. If we don't, they simply outgrow their faith. I am working to change the trend and raise the bar here!

Cliff

Currently, we are not raising up a generation of soldiers ready for spiritual battle. We treat youth like children rather than as young adults who are preparing for lifelong service to God. Youth will rise to the level that spiritual leaders set for them.

The North American Mission Board reports that 88 percent of churched youth drop out of church when they finish high school. That's not exactly the rite of passage we seek. Barna's statistics are only slightly better: "Barely one-third of white and Hispanic teens, along with two-fifths of black teens, say they are likely to continue to attend a Christian church in the future, while they are living independently of their parents."[6]

But I sense a new wind blowing. My wife, Michelle, loves the Weather Channel. She watches it with great devotion, and could probably fill in as a guest meteorologist at a local TV station. Her interest in weather comes in handy, as in our eight years in North Carolina we've faced two hurricanes, some horrendous ice storms, a severe drought one year, and severe flooding another. Hurricanes, though, are the most fascinating. Several natural forces converge at just the right time—or if you're in the path of the storm, the wrong time.

As in the development of a hurricane, several forces currently seem to be converging on the church at about the same time. *First,* over the past several years I've met literally hundreds of youth pastors all over the nation, and they feel much the same—they love youth ministry and youth, but are frustrated with the current state of youth ministry. Many recognize the need for a reformation of youth ministry, yet most I meet have more questions than answers.

The *second* force is the new generation, the Millennials.

The *third* force arises from my generation. A growing, foaming, tsunami of parental passion has expressed itself recently in an explosion of everything from Christian and home schools, to countless parenting seminars, to the rise of Dr. Laura, to the Amber Alert system when a child is abducted. Parents of youth and preteens want to get it right with their kids.

The *fifth* and *final* force comes from what we know about God. The forces above are not lost on our great God. He was not caught by surprise at Columbine or on 9-11, and He is well aware of coming trends. In the past, God has used generations of young people in times of great revival. Might He be preparing a new generation to use in similar fashion?

One thing is certain. God *is* at work. Will we, like Barnabas in Acts 11, seek to see the hand of God in a new generation? By perpetuating the status quo, or by ignoring the evidence, or by failing to seek Him for wisdom, do we honor God and help a generation?

Teenagers have power today. Barna gives examples:
- Teenagers largely define the values and leisure endeavors of our nation.
- The family is the foundation of the universe, and much in society is impacted on how youth prioritize the family.
- Finally, the future of the church will be determined by this generation's faith and commitments.[7]

The good news is that a large number of young people attend church youth groups—about one-third of America's teens, according to Barna.[8] The bad news is that the rise of youth ministry over the last generation has failed to produce spiritual giants. As noted earlier, if anything, the impact of youth ministry has dropped in recent years. Barna observes, "While youth ministry has become a standard ministry program in tens of thousands of churches . . . there has been surprisingly little growth in the involvement of teenagers in the life of the Church over the past decade."[9]

John Detonni makes this point: "Most often youth workers—and especially youth pastors—are very pragmatic and oriented to the program. Fun and games, Bible studies, camps, retreats, social activities, and such things. It is a little difficult to talk about philosophy and theology with such youth workers in the morning when they know they are taking care of 15 junior highers that same evening. Further, youth workers have a reputation of not being 'thinkers' but doers, being more interested in how to do youth ministry than the reasons and basis of it."[10]

A Personal Journey into Youth Ministry

Years ago psychologist Abraham Maslow developed what he called a hierarchy of needs. Everyone—no matter what background, nationality, or economic situation—has certain needs, such as food, shelter, and a sense of safety. Maslow was right but didn't go far enough. Everyone also has another need—to know God and to make a difference with her or his God-given life. Mathematician Blaise Pascal describes that need as a God-sized vacuum, or a God-shaped hole as an Audio Adrenaline song put it. Only Jesus can fill that hole. He does more, however, than fill it. He gives each person who receives Him a passion to live out God's purpose.

I was reminded of this at a DiscipleNow gathering that I led. About 225 teenagers met for a weekend at a church near Atlanta, Georgia. This weekend was different, however, from others the church had held. Instead of taking the youth miles away to a big extravaganza and playing games, the weekend featured large-group times with expository preaching, a day filled with intentional personal evangelism, and much time spent in prayer and self-examination. You may think laser tag would have been more fun, but the students *loved* it! So much so that the one extra event, a contemporary Christian concert, was postponed on Friday night because God had stirred the youth so profoundly in the large-group time that preceded the concert.

The large-group times featured no games, just some excellent praise and worship followed by a serious message, that lasted thirty-five to forty-five minutes. After each session the students went into small groups that focused on serious self-examination.

On Saturday, students did evangelism projects—from giving away bread or batteries for smoke detectors, to visiting nursing homes, to cleaning toilets. While doing these tasks the students shared Christ and gave away tracts. The students got so excited that many begged to keep witnessing even when the scheduled time was up.

Over twenty-five students met Christ that weekend. And nearly all the students made a public commitment—including signing their names—to pray daily and intensively for twenty-eight days following the weekend.

Following the weekend, a public school principal called the student minister—not to complain—but to ask what had happened to the students. He saw a clear difference in the teens who had gone to the weekend, and he loved the change. God continued to work in the students for weeks following that weekend.

That weekend illustrates one premise of *Raising the Bar*. When students begin to understand God's purpose for their lives—which comes through devotion to His Word, through intentional prayer, and by telling others about Jesus—they learn that serving Christ is far from boring. Students did not complain during that weekend; they rejoiced in their opportunity to honor God.

There were three keys to the success of that weekend. *First,* prior to the weekend, leaders prayed intensively for four weeks, following a twenty-eight-day prayer guide. The weekend was then followed by a twenty-eight-day prayer commitment from the students.[11] When we pray, God works.

Second, the focus was not on games but on God, not on playing but on God's purposes. Preaching was given preeminence over activities. Games are not evil, and they have their place, but they are inferior to the joy of pleasing Jesus.

Third, evangelism was given priority. The youth at this church, like most teens, had no special abilities or gifts. Many had never witnessed before and were very nervous. God used them, and He will use us to lead them, despite our weaknesses. Often the great saints in history, and even well-known spiritual leaders today, are presented as larger than life, as if they had some kind of holy glitter showered on them. But they are normal people whom God chose to use mightily. They made mistakes, struggled with sin, and served God in spite of their weaknesses. You and I are just as much children of God as they are. We have the same Jesus, the same love of God, and a purpose from God. Why not take a group of teens at your church, go out in the community, and share the love of Jesus? It could be awesome!

In Deuteronomy 30, Moses addresses the nation of Israel at a critical time. Nearing the day of crossing into the Promised Land, the new postwilderness generation needed firm spiritual footing on which to tread. Moses challenged the people with these words: "I have set before you life and death, blessing and cursing; therefore choose life . . ." (v. 19).

The people of God stood at a crossroads, and so do we. We stand at the brink of the world of postmodernism. We are not leaving the wilderness; we are entering it—a world of relativism, pluralism, and tolerance. As you stand before a new generation, challenge them to choose life— the life found in Jesus. Challenge them to follow His way and embrace His truth.

Chapter Three

The Potency of Expectancy

Why We Can Be Optimistic

Now those who were scattered after the persecution that arose over Stephen traveled as far as Phoenicia, Cyprus, and Antioch, preaching the word to no one but the Jews only. But some of them were men from Cyprus and Cyrene, who, when they had come to Antioch, spoke to the Hellenists, preaching the Lord Jesus. And the hand of the Lord was with them, and a great number believed and turned to the Lord.

Then news of these things came to the ears of the church in Jerusalem, and they sent out Barnabas to go as far as Antioch. When he came and had seen the grace of God, he was glad, and encouraged them all that with purpose of heart they should continue with the Lord. For he was a good man, full of the Holy Spirit and of faith. And a great many people were added to the Lord.

—Acts 11:19–24

What do the following people have in common?

- Cassie Bernall
- Jim Elliot
- Timothy McVeigh
- Osama Bin Laden

Cassie Bernall was martyred at Columbine in 1999; Elliot was martyred by the Auca Indians in Ecuador in the 1950s; McVeigh and

Bin Laden are terrorists, both responsible for the massacre of multitudes of innocent Americans. But, yes, all four have much in common. They share one characteristic that most people lack—*they're all radicals.*

It's a radical thing to blow up a federal building as McVeigh did. It's a radical thing to enlist and inspire a group of men, as Bin Laden did, to kill thousands in a suicide mission. It's also a radical thing to stand for Jesus in your high school and take a bullet. It's a radical thing to allow natives—the very natives whom you seek to win to Christ—to spear you to death.

History has been changed more by radicals than by diplomats. The difference between Bernall and Elliot on the one hand and the terrorists on the other is the focus of their radical convictions. Imagine what would happen if thousands of young people in America served Jesus with the passion of a Bin Laden? Imagine if high school youth spent as much time planning to reach their peers with the gospel as McVeigh spent planning his bomb attack?

Such a scenario is far from impossible with this generation of youth. Consider the ten characteristics listed in chapter 1 that describe in general today's youngsters. And perhaps never in American history have youth in the *church* been more poised to penetrate the culture. Churches report observing the same characteristics in Millennials as observed by Howe and Strauss. The weeks following the disaster in Littleton, Colorado, the Internet, e-mail, Christian clubs, and church youth groups witnessed a surge in spiritual fervor. Since 1990—when the Supreme Court allowed prayer clubs to meet on public school property, provided they met outside class hours and without adult leadership—an explosion of Bible clubs by the thousands occurred across this country. The clubs have culminated most recently in the rise of First Priority clubs, which are spreading across the nation like a Kansas grass fire.

These youth denote a new breed of evangelical Christians. Barnard College religion professor Randall Balmer says,

> Unlike their evangelical parents, who often defined themselves as outsiders, today's campus Christians are willing to engage the

culture on its terms. They understand what's going on and speak the language. Teen evangelicals have their own rock concert circuit, complete with stage diving; their own clothing lines, like Witness Wear; and in the omnipresent WWJD ("What Would Jesus Do?") bracelet, their own bracelet accessory.

And now their own martyr[s].[1]

This generation certainly faces challenges, as every generation does. In the 1960s, when I was in grade school, the great fear was nuclear destruction. Bomb shelters were the rage, and civil defense drills were as common as fire drills. Today, few children fear a nuclear holocaust, yet they still fear, and the thing they fear is violent crime. Terrorism has hit home, and civil defense drills have been replaced by lockdown drills in case a madman invades a school.

Many young people don't know which way to turn for help. As I watched news reports following the Columbine shooting, I found myself nodding in agreement with an FBI agent's comments: "We once had the family, the church, and the school working together. Now all that's left is the school, and it's not enough."

Focusing on the challenges, however, and neglecting the positive signs around us help no one. Barry St. Clair, president of Reach Out Ministries, reminds us of something that most churches have forgotten: "Students have awesome potential to change their world."[2]

As I write this, my son, Josh, is moving from middle school to high school. He's already led many people to Christ in personal evangelism, he plays in the "adult" praise band at church, he knows more Scripture than many seminary students. He still acts his age or younger at times, but he finds his fulfillment in spending time with people years his senior and in activities many "adult" believers avoid (like evangelism). Why? Because that's the bar that's been set for him, and the example that he's seen, and the encouragement that he's been given.

Perhaps it would be worthy of our Lord and helpful to our children to explore ways we can affect the Millennial generation while they're still so open to guidance and change.

> Barna gives three marks of this generation:
> 1. They will be the most numerous generation in America's history;
> 2. They will likely baffle millions of people with their unpredictable, quixotic, and seemingly inconsistent and idiosyncratic values, beliefs, attitudes, and behaviors;
> 3. Mosaics will provide the church with a massive and fertile population for evangelism and discipleship.[3]

A young man named Charles, while precocious, demonstrated many of the insecurities typical of youth. But on a dreary, winter day marked by blizzard conditions, he was determined to go to church. He made it to a little Methodist church, where the minister didn't even come because the weather was so bad. So a deacon preached to the handful huddled at the meeting. In the course of his sermon, the deacon fixed his eyes on young Charles and said, "Look to Jesus!" The words seared the very soul of young Charles.

That youth did look to Jesus, and a few years later became the pastor of the great Metropolitan Tabernacle in London. That young man, Charles Haddon Spurgeon, became one of the greatest preachers of all time.

Spurgeon is just one example of youth making a difference. He was moved to do so by the challenge of a church leader. We adults today also need to heed the exhortation of that deacon and look to Jesus as we challenge our youth. Such a view leads us to courage rather than cowardice, to hope over despair, to faith instead of doubt.

The earliest believers demonstrated the capacity to see the potential for God's work in the most unlikely places. In Acts 3, for example, immediately following the incredible movement of God at Pentecost, Peter and John encountered a lame man. Acts 4 tells us that this man, lame from birth, was over forty years of age. With no wheelchairs, no Americans with Disabilities Act, no special programs for those with disabilities, the lame man was totally dependent upon others to carry him to a place where, daily, he begged for food. If the heat parched his tongue, he could not go for water. If the cold brought him discomfort, he could not plug in an electric blanket.

So he lay there, by the temple, where Peter and John saw him. No doubt the lame man had heard of the stir caused by these Galileans. So he looked at them, expecting to receive something.

Generally, God's level of blessing rises to our level of expectancy. Sometimes, God's blessing far exceeds our hopes and dreams. The lame man sought alms and, through Peter and John, God gave to him new legs. The lame man sought temporal help and God gave to him eternal life.

Most everyone saw the lame man as a liability. Yet the healing of this man—and Peter's preaching that followed—led to a larger harvest for the gospel than occurred at Pentecost (Acts 4:4). Could it be that we've missed seeing the hand of God at work because we haven't seen the potential of youth? It's time to stop seeing youth as a liability in the church and begin seeing them as central to the activity of God in our day.

In Acts 11 a movement of God changed the city of Antioch. Persecution forced regular believers out of Jerusalem, scattering witnesses everywhere. A group of believers went to Antioch, and God honored their witness, saving many. Barnabas, the encourager, was sent to Antioch to provide leadership to the fledgling church there.

Barnabas began in Antioch with a new generation of Christians, and it's easy to imagine that he saw the potential for God's work. He started from scratch, and built a church that eventually would send out the first missionaries (see Acts 13). He led people who had no previous knowledge of the gospel to a remarkable level of ministry. You and I have the same opportunity with the Millennial generation.

A Dose of Perspective

Have you ever been so close to a situation that you couldn't see change occurring? Josh had a severe case of lazy eye when he was a baby. One of his eyes turned, and wouldn't move in tandem with the other. But Michelle and I didn't see it. How was it detected? My parents came for a visit and, since they hadn't seen Josh for several months, noticed it immediately. Once they pointed it out, it became obvious to us, too. In the same way, it's possible to be too close to youth ministry to see what God is doing with a new generation.

Susan Partridge has been a missionary in Asia for many years. She observes a marked change in the attitude of students from her last furlough in 1997–1998 to her recent one in 2001–2002. "Students now are remarkably more interested in missions. They want to give their lives in service to the Lord," she told me. This is exactly what I've observed the past few years. When I speak to students, my message is very simple: be a radical. And young people are responding to that challenge like never before.

The change is noticeable in China, as well. Susan noted the interest in contemporary Christian music (CCM) on the part of both the churched and unchurched youth in China. A growing body of praise and worship music is also a phenomena in that country.

In his ministry with thousands of students over many years, Greg Stier observes this about the current generation:

> As I travel the nation, I encounter teenagers everywhere who are sick and tired of typical church and dying instead for authentic Christianity. Students all over the nation are crying out for something real. They want a driving cause to live for, and if necessary, to die for. They are tired of the traditional. They long for the radical. . . . They must be energized, equipped, and turned loose with the life-changing, culture-transforming, world-shaking message of the Gospel of Jesus Christ. No frills. No games. No wimps. Just contagious, unstoppable Christian students.[4]

The International Mission Board of the Southern Baptist Convention recently began encouraging mission teams of young people to flood the mission field on short-term mission trips. The flood abated for a brief time after 9-11, but because of parents, not because of the youth. The board's shift in philosophy recognizes both an awareness of the awesome potential of teens, and that God is raising up a new generation.

Such recognition is long overdue, but we as parents and youth pastors must also recognize what stands in the way of youth achieving their potential. The greatest enemy facing youth today is not other teens or worldliness. The greatest threat to young people is adults. Think about it:

- The media preys on them, glorifying for sheer profit the most extreme lifestyle choices sexually, musically, and relationally. When he was head of MTV, Bob Pittman said, "We don't seek fourteen-year-olds; we own them."[5]
- Divorce robs youth of their greatest need, which is not financial abundance or social status but a loving home environment.
- Abuse threatens them.
- Neglect destroys them.

I was camp pastor for a church in Plano, Texas, in the 1980s. Plano led the nation in the number of teen suicides at the time—and I soon found out why. Students told me of the extreme opulence, including helicopter and private jet rides to the senior prom. At the same time, they attended massive public schools where they felt like numbers. Their dads were, for the most part, absent, pursuing the material possessions they provided. The teens received everything that their parents wanted them to have; what they didn't get from their parents was what they most needed—encouragement to live passionately for Jesus.

Young people today enjoy leisure time just like earlier generations. But they take more seriously education as well as other factors that will help them to make an impact in their world. "Four out of every 10 teenagers named the challenges related to educational achievement as their top focus," Barna found. "This reflects a major transition from just a few years ago."[6] The bottom line in Barna's findings is that the number one concern of teenagers is the potential to succeed in life.

The youthful years, then, are the most important window of opportunity to teach teens the features of Christianity that matter. Youth are not the church of tomorrow; they are the church of today!

Michael Lewis reports in his book, *Next: The Future Just Happened,* "If people haven't tried a new kind of food, like, say, Japanese food, by the time they're twenty-five years old, there's a 99 percent chance that they won't try it for the rest of their lives. If they haven't tried a new kind of fashion by the time they're twenty, like an earring or a nose ring, there's a 99 percent chance that they'll never do it for the rest of their lives."[7]

The Church of Jesus Christ-Latter Day Saints, or Mormonism, began in the 1800s, spreading around the world in less than two centuries. From an objective, research perspective, the growth of Mormonism has been remarkable. The Jesus preached in Mormonism is not, however, the Jesus of the Bible. Mormonism demonstrates that effective methodology, even when matched with aberrant theology, can be used to reach a host of people.

Mormons understand, too, the power of youth. Some of my students who came to Christ out of Mormonism have told me some pertinent details. When a child is born to a devout Mormon home, a bank account is opened. Year after year money is invested in that account. The child is reminded continuously of the purpose of the investment—the Mormon mission. This grueling, two-year mission, paid for by the youth and their families, follows a rigorous schedule: 6:00 A.M.—prayer and study; visitation until late that night, with a one-hour dinner break. Further, they cannot communicate with family or friends by phone, fax, or e-mail, with only two exceptions: Mother's Day and Christmas.[8]

Stier recognizes the significant impact of the mission: "They leave [home] as boys. They come back as men. They know what they believe and why they believe it. Their theology has been hammered out on doorsteps. Their resolve has been tested and strengthened by thousands of slammed doors, barking dogs, rainy days, and mocking looks."[9]

The church—ministry in general, youth ministry, parents—has the opportunity to set a new standard for young people, to encourage their involvement in the Christian movement. Do our current methods demonstrate that we anticipate greatness? There is potency in expectancy—let's expect great things!

Chapter Four

Truth or Consequences

Biblical Teaching Confronts Contemporary Practice

And Jesus increased in wisdom and stature, and in favor with God and men.

—Luke 2:52

Young people today will not listen to a message longer than seventeen minutes." This statement was made recently to youth pastors at a conference sponsored by a nationally known youth leader. A youth pastor I know was there. He told the so-called expert, "I'll need to apologize to my students—for bringing them to a conference where the very leader of the conference so disrespects them."

The conference leader's misguided notion ignores the capacity of students to sit through movies or class, or even wait in lines at theme parks. Worse, it shows contempt toward the power of the Holy Spirit, the Word of God, and the place of preaching in the Christian church. It is yet another example of treating students like children, not young adults.

As has been shown, history records stirring examples of young people serving the Lord, but the church today has not taken seriously the need to equip students theologically. This failure has led to under-challenged and under-trained youth. Many studies demonstrate a further result over the past generation: the erosion of theological conviction among college students in evangelical schools.[1]

Part of this chapter comes from Alvin L. Reid, "From Northampton to Columbine: Understanding the Potential of Young People for the Contemporary Church," address to the Evangelical Theological Society, Colorado Springs, Colorado, November 14, 2001.

A Biblical Perspective: The Myth of Adolescence

My colleague and a Greek scholar, David Alan Black, has allowed me to use the title of his book *The Myth of Adolescence* to make my point. "What," Black asks, "do the Scriptures say about adolescence? *Absolutely nothing.*"[2] Moses, Paul, John, and others went from childhood to adulthood. Were they ever teenagers? Yes. But they were never adolescents. Black argues that, biblically, there are three stages to one's life:

1. Childhood/pre-adulthood (ages one to twelve)
2. Emerging adulthood (ages twelve to thirty)
3. Senior adulthood (age thirty to death)[3]

Black notes that these stages can be seen in the life of Jesus (Luke 2:41–52; 3:23; and the remainder of the Gospel, respectively) and in the persons John describes in his first epistle ("little children," "young people," and "fathers"). The transitions are significant: puberty at age twelve, and the move to responsible adulthood at about age thirty. Notice the absence of a separate category of teenage years.

The Old Testament denotes other categories. In the Pentateuch, for example, men twenty and older were fit for war (see Num. 26), and only those twenty and older could give an offering (Exod. 30:14). While these and other distinctives are found in the Old Covenant, Black's argument stands: the Bible mentions nothing of the separate place of the teen years. Nor does it mention the concomitant expectation of adolescent behavior, which expectation is so prevalent in American culture, including in the church.

Black argues, and I would agree, that there's no biblical warrant for the concept of adolescence. Yet that concept has led to an entire subculture of youth ministry—well intentioned but too often poorly founded— as well as the remarkable growth of so-called family ministries in the church.

> According to the Bible, the teen era is not a "time-out" between childhood and adulthood. It is not primarily a time of horse-play. . . . The Bible treats teens as responsible adults, and so

should we. Paul told Timothy, a young man, "Don't let anyone look down on you because you are young. Instead, be an example for other believers in your speech, behavior, love, faith, and purity" (1 Tim. 4:12).[4]

Does this mean youth are to be prohibited from enjoying times of innocent, carefree play? Certainly not. But the idea of suspending life for a multiyear period of silliness is . . . well . . . silliness.

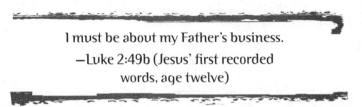

I must be about my Father's business.
—Luke 2:49b (Jesus' first recorded words, age twelve)

The concept of adolescence has led our culture, both inside and outside the church, to fabricate two myths about youth. First, it encourages teenagers to behave like grade-school children instead of young adults. Second, it perpetuates the notion that the teenage years are, of necessity, a time of rebellion, sarcasm, narcissism, and general evildoing. "Sowing wild oats" has become a popular term for what is expected of youth— including churched youth—during their young adult days. Certainly the hormonal changes and rapid maturation taking place in adolescence may, if left unchecked, result in such behavior. But that's my point: we mustn't let the bar of expectation be set so low.

More and more voices are sounding a challenge to the notion of adolescence. Soon after Columbine, *Time* magazine featured a back-page article that calls into question the way society as a whole has treated young people in recent generations. Lance Morrow observes,

Humans . . . have turned the long stretch from puberty to autonomy into a suspended state of simultaneous overindulgence and neglect. American adolescence tends to be disconnected from the adult world and from the functioning expectation . . . of entering that world and assuming a responsible place there. The word *adolescence* means, literally, growing up. No growing up occurs if there is nothing to grow up to. Without the adult connection, adolescence becomes a Neverland, a Mall of Lost Children.[5]

In the *Time* article, Morrow referred to an op-ed piece by Leon Botstein, president of Bard College, that appeared the week before in the *New York Times*. Botstein suggested, "The American High School is obsolete and should be abolished." Morrow added, "At sixteen, young Americans are prepared to be taken seriously. . . . They need to enter a world where they are not in a lunchroom only with their peers." Morrow then offers a fascinating opinion coming from the mainstream, secular media:

> Maybe we should abolish adolescence altogether. Not the biological part. . . . We are stuck with that. But it would be nice if we could get rid of the cultural mess we have made of the teenage years. Having deprived children of an innocent childhood, the least we would do is rescue them from an adolescence corrupted by every sleazy, violent and commercially lucrative fantasy that untrammeled adult venality, high-horsing on the First Amendment, can conceive.[6]

Morrow notes a scene in J. D. Salinger's *Catcher in the Rye* (1951)—a book he calls "one of the founding documents of American adolescence." Holden Caulfield is a young man who was expelled from a prep school. After donning a red hat, Caulfield was asked by a kid whether it was a deer shooting hat. Squinting as if aiming to shoot, Caulfield replied, "This is a people shooting hat. I shoot people in it."[7] A generation later, life has imitated art.

Black cites an article by David Bakan that notes three origins of adolescence theory. First, compulsory education laws were passed that changed the centuries-old process of parents teaching their children, putting education into the hands of the state. Second, child labor laws were passed that made it illegal for persons to work before a certain age. While aimed no doubt at protecting children, the laws served to take away responsibilities from many who were ready to take them. Finally, the juvenile justice system was created to separate younger lawbreakers from older ones.[8] Thus, the twentieth century saw the rise of adolescence, accompanied by a plethora of supporting organizations: public schools, Boy Scouts and Girl Scouts, boys' and girls' agricultural clubs, and youth ministry. Black's summation of the results is telling:

> It is my conviction that the social theory of adolescence undermines both the Christian understanding of human nature and the way in which Christians analyze moral thought. [That theory] underscores the modern disinclination to treat a person as responsible for his or her actions. When we assert the "fact" that children are to act like children rather than like adults, [theory] becomes a self-fulfilling prophecy.[9]

Thus my generation has produced a president of the United States who can conduct the affairs of state with world leaders (mature behavior) while having an affair (adolescent behavior) with a young intern. It also produced Michael Jackson, one of the biggest pop icons ever. At age forty-five, Jackson says he wishes he were Peter Pan and has spent a fortune in a pathetic attempt to turn his home into Never Never Land—where, by the way, children are told they never have to grow up.

While there are obvious differences between someone who is fifteen and someone who is twenty-five, I agree with Black that teens can be responsible young adults if given the chance. Further, they can be prepared to be used by God while still in their teens. If teens can learn trigonometry, calculus, and advanced chemistry, they can learn theology!

As Black maintains, then, the Bible issues no warrant for the concept of adolescence. And, as he further notes, the concept has obviously not worked. What, then, does the Bible say about youth?

Biblical Models

While the Bible does not consign youth to a separate, adolescent category as is done today, it does speak often about young adults. A reading of the entire Bible with an eye to what it says about youth finds that the vast majority of references to youth depicts them in a positive light.

Certainly the young men mocking Elisha, the youths who give bad advice to Rehoboam, and Eli's wicked sons are negative examples, but these few examples pale in comparison to the many godly, noble, and often heroic youth.

- *Joseph.* As a seventeen-year-old, Joseph's own family sold him into slavery; the wife of the man (Potiphar) who showed Joseph kindness tried to seduce him; he wound up in jail because he said no; others abused him and victimized him. Yet Joseph continued to trust God, and God used Joseph to preserve His people. Knowing His people would face tremendous famine in the future, God used the tragic circumstances of a seventeen-year-old. God moved Joseph into a place of leadership, where he provided for Israel when, years later, a famine came.
- *Samuel.* At a time when the word of God was rare, the boy Samuel heard the voice of God. God saw that the sons of Eli the priest were evil, unfit to continue to minister to the Lord. At that time He heard the cries of a barren woman named Hannah and gave her a son, whom she named Samuel. Samuel would become one of the great spiritual leaders.
- *David.* When King Saul proved unfit as a leader, God took a shepherd boy named David and made him a great king.

I could cite the examples of Esther, Daniel and his friends, Rhoda, and Timothy. And let us not overlook even our Lord. Remember the first recorded words of Jesus? "I must be about my Father's business." That's a good standard for anyone. His age at the time? He was twelve!

What the Bible teaches makes clear what we've overlooked—God uses youth. He is sovereign over the universe, and knows tomorrow's headlines *yesterday.* Even youth leaders forget this at times. Imagine, then, what great things those headlines of tomorrow might say about the youth of today. The time is ripe to remind ourselves of Jesus' standard, and to lead students to be about the Father's business.

Chapter Five

Entertaining Children or Assembling an Army

Lessons from History

But My servant Caleb, because he has a different spirit in him and has followed Me fully, I will bring into the land where he went, and his descendants shall inherit it.
—Numbers 14:24

Next.
This simple moniker served as the introduction by *ESPN the Magazine* for Lebron James. James averaged over thirty points a game for Saint Vincent-Saint Mary's in Akron, Ohio, in 2002–2003. Never in history has such hype been given to a high school senior. At age eighteen, James—considered by some to be good enough to start on every NBA team—is one of many examples of America's sports world increasingly finding itself led by younger and younger athletes. All the talk on sports radio and in print about whether such young athletes are being taken advantage of misses an important point: young athletes are not only a part of the sports picture, they're setting the agenda for college athletics.

In 2002, the University of North Carolina began its season with an unprecedented starting lineup: three freshmen, along with two sophomores. Major universities, which once refused to allow freshmen to play their first year, now depend increasingly on younger players. Doing so is, ostensibly, to get the most out of talented athletes before they turn pro early. This explanation, however, accounts for only a small percentage of the freshmen who make their way into starting lineups. Another explanation is that many freshmen today are, at age eighteen, far more skilled than were their counterparts thirty years ago. This reasoning is hard to argue with considering that, when Lebron James' team played the Oak Hill Academy, the game filled a thirteen-thousand-seat arena and gave ESPN2 one of its best ratings ever (for a *high school* game). In addition, the ten starters were all headed for Division I schools—except for James, who was heading for the number one pick in the NBA draft. Some high school academies could, in fact, beat college teams.

At the collegiate athletic level, coaches are clearly discovering what the church has missed: you can lean on young people to respond correctly, even heroically, in high-pressure situations. The church, however, has forgotten this truth.

If We Don't Learn from History, We Will Repeat Its Mistakes

Santayana offers some sage advice: those who fail to learn from history are doomed to repeat its failures. The same advice is offered here, but with a twist: those who fail to note the impact of youth in history are doomed to miss the potential of youth today.

As noted, history records the most remarkable, God-driven spiritual awakenings are often inspired by young people. In some cases, the maturity of the seasoned has channeled the zeal of youth into leadership. Jonathan Edwards, J. Edwin Orr, and other historians of awakening have noted the vital role of young people in great revival. We must recapture this understanding today!

Looking to biblical history one also notes shifts in generational attitudes. Prior to entering the Promised Land, for example, an entire generation abandoned faith and died in the wilderness. A new era unfolded, however, with the children of Israel's entrance into the land. Only Joshua and Caleb represented the previous time. The book of Numbers gives insight into why Caleb was allowed to enter the Promised Land. Caleb had, of course, given a good report, as did Joshua, when both were included in the original party of spies. But Numbers 14:24 adds this insight: "But my servant Caleb, because he had a different spirit in him and has followed me fully, I will bring into the land where he went, and his descendants shall inherit it."

Little wonder, then, that the psalmist charged elders to teach the coming generation to follow the Lord (Ps. 78:1–7). From his youth, Caleb (and by inference Joshua) was instilled with a "different spirit" from that of the rest of his generation.

The Millennial generation certainly has a different spirit—not necessarily one that follows the Lord as did Caleb, but one that marks a clear departure from those before it. Generations of youth between Caleb and Millennials have also been marked by a different spirit.

Historically: The Zeal of Youth

Paul told Timothy not to let anyone look down on him because of his youth.[1] But that's not all he said. He exhorted Timothy to *be an example* in speech (a strong argument against a separate youth "lingo"), in behavior, love, faith, and purity (1 Tim. 4:12). Paul apparently believed a young man could be a leader.

As stated earlier, the most overlooked aspect of modern revival movements or awakenings is the role played by young people. Recall that Jonathan Edwards recorded on more than one occasion that the First Great Awakening was, more than anything, a youth movement. Yet in most cases, while the primary sources of history tend to convey one message, the role of youth has been neglected in secondary sources of history.

Pietism

Pietism was a late seventeenth-century reform movement beginning in the Lutheran Church and spreading to other groups. After the Reformation many Lutheran churches became spiritually dead. Thus, some, like Philip Spener, sought to reform the church, and young people played no small role. Most historians date the beginning of Pietism with the publication of Philip Spener's *Pia Desideria* ("Pious Desires") in 1675.[2] Spener, called the Father of Pietism by many, emphasized the personal nature of the Christian experience. He led many small-group Bible studies that spread across parts of Europe, and many young people attended the meetings.

Young people, too, at university helped spread the fervor of Pietism. Spener secured the appointment of A. H. Francke at the new University of Halle in 1692. Under Francke's leadership Halle became "a pietistic center of higher education and revivalism."[3] Francke not only taught theology, but he took the young people out into the community to do hands-on ministry.

Nicholaus Ludwig Von Zinzendorf (1700–1760) studied at Halle from 1710 to 1716. Zinzendorf organized prayer groups among the students while at the university.[4] From Halle, Zinzendorf went to the University of Wittenberg, where in 1718 he formed the Order of the Grain of Mustard Seed. In 1722 he acquired an estate that became a safe haven for persecuted members of the Hussite church. It was from this group that the "Unitas Fratrum" (Unity of the Brethren), or Moravians, was born. A particularly powerful movement of the Spirit came at a communion service on August 12, 1727. Following this, a continuous prayer structure developed, resulting in a missionary enterprise that saw one in every sixty Moravians' becoming a missionary. Clearly, Zinzendorf's impact was significant and can be traced to his teen years at Halle.

The Evangelical Awakening in England

John Wesley (1703–1791) and George Whitefield (1714–1770) were two leaders of the Evangelical Awakening in England during the eighteenth century.[5] Wesley's experience as a college student at Oxford is probably best remembered by the "Holy Club," which involved John, his brother Charles Wesley, Whitefield, and a handful of others. Whitefield was converted during those days. That John Wesley was not actually converted until years after his Oxford days does not minimize the impact made by the Holy Club on his subsequent ministry.

The Holy Club experience forged relationships between the young men, who later figured prominently in the awakening in England and the American colonies. Wesley's often-cited conversion in 1738 led to a remarkable ministry, which, along with Whitefield's influence and Charles' hymn writing, affected the spiritual life of the entire nation. While never desiring to sever ties with the Church of England, the Evangelical Awakening resulted in the formation of the Methodist Church.

By 1791, the year of John Wesley's death, 79,000 Methodist churches had been established in England.

Its Spread to the New World

Beyond his impact in England, Whitefield made seven trips to the New World. His itinerant ministry across the colonies helped to fan the flames of local revivals into the inferno of the Great Awakening. What makes Whitefield's influence more impressive is that he was only twenty-six years old when the Great Awakening was at its peak.

The first of a series of revival movements during the course of Jonathan Edwards' Northampton ministry was the Valley Revival of 1734–1735. Edwards referred to the role of the youth in its origin: "At the latter end of the year 1733, there appeared a very unusual flexibleness, and yielding to advice, in our young people."[6] This came after Edwards began speaking against their irreverence toward the Sabbath. At the same time youth were also greatly affected by the sudden death of a young man and then of a young married woman in their town. Edwards, recognizing an opportunity to change young hearts, proposed that the young people should begin meeting in small groups around Northampton. They did so with such success that many adults followed their example.

Edwards stressed that awakenings were not only inspired and led by young people, they particularly affected the younger generation. Speaking about the effect of the First Great Awakening on youth, he wrote, "God made it, I suppose, the greatest occasion of awakening to others, of anything that ever came to pass in the town. News of it seemed to be almost like a flash of lightning, upon the hearts of young people, all over town, and upon many others."[7] This revival, which erupted in his town of Northampton, Massachusetts, spread quickly to neighboring towns and greatly affected all.

Beyond the impact the awakening had on young people, it must be noted that most of the leaders of the revival were touched by God personally while young. Edwards himself while still a child began his passionate pursuit of God, and his precocious spiritual zeal was obvious in his teen years. The First Great Awakening would include the work, too, of George Whitefield, in his twenties at the height of his influence. Several leaders in the First Great Awakening arose from the Log College of

Presbyterian William Tennent. Tennent's log house, built to provide ministerial training for three of his sons and fifteen others, made no small mark on the leadership development of ministers during the awakening.[8] After visiting the Tennent family in Pennsylvania, George Whitefield recorded the following in his journal:

> The place wherein the young men study now is in contempt called The College. It is a log house, about twenty feet long and near as many broad; and to me it seemed to resemble the school of the old prophets, for their habitations were mean. . . . From this despised place, seven or eight worthy ministers of Jesus have lately been sent forth; more are almost ready to be sent, and the foundation is now laying for the instruction of many others.[9]

Leaders from The College in the First Great Awakening included Tenant's sons Gilbert—the most prominent revival leader among Presbyterians—John, and William Jr., along with Samuel Blair. In addition, many graduates established log colleges of their own. The Log College, which ultimately evolved into the College of New Jersey (now Princeton University), has been called "the forerunner of modern seminaries."[10]

At the turn of the nineteenth century the Second Great Awakening spread across the emerging United States. A major precipitating factor in this movement was the outbreak of revival on college campuses. Skepticism and infidelity, influenced by European thinkers, characterized especially eastern colleges during this period immediately following the birth of the United States.

The campus of Hampden-Sydney College in Virginia experienced the first in a series of college revivals, and the fertile field of young students played a pivotal role. Four young men—William Hill, Carey Allen, James Blythe, and Clement Read—were instrumental in the beginnings of revival at Hampden-Sydney in 1787 and the years following. Because they feared severe antagonism from the irreligious student body, the four young men began meeting secretly in the forest to pray and study. When they were discovered, they were greatly ridiculed by fellow students.

Note, though, what happened when John Blair Smith provided appropriate guidance. Smith, the college president, heard of the situation and was convicted by the infidelity on the campus. He invited the four students and others to pray with him in his parlor, arguably an instance of youth ministry. Before long, revival spread rapidly through the college and to surrounding counties. Hill later chronicled the revival's impact:

> Persons of all ranks in society, of all ages . . . became subjects of this work, so that there was scarcely a Magistrate on the bench, or a lawyer at the bar but became members of the church. . . . It was now as rare a thing to find one who was not religious, as it was formerly to find one that was. *The frivolities and amusements once so prevalent were all abandoned, and gave place to singing, serious conversations, and prayer meetings.*[11] (emphasis added)

In addition, subsequent revival movements came in 1802, 1814–1815, 1822, 1827–1828, 1831, 1833, and 1837.[12]

The Yale College revival began under the leadership of President Timothy Dwight, the grandson of Jonathan Edwards. When Dwight came to Yale, it was filled with infidelity. He began to preach against unbelief in the college chapel, and by 1797 a group of students formed to improve moral conditions. After much prayer, a powerful spiritual movement permeated the school in the spring of 1802. A third of the student body was converted, and Goodrich wrote of the change in attitude on campus: "The salvation of the soul was the great subject of thought, of conversation, of absorbing interest; the convictions of many were pungent and overwhelming; and 'the peace of believing' which succeeded, was not less strongly marked."[13] The movement spread to Dartmouth and Princeton, at Princeton three-fourths of the students making professions and one-fourth entering the ministry.[14]

A group of students at Williams College in Massachusetts made a tremendous impact on missions. Samuel Mills entered the college during a time of awakening there between 1804 and 1806. He and four others began to pray regularly for missions, and in 1806 at one particular meeting they had to seek refuge from the rain in a haystack. During this "Haystack Meeting," Mills proposed a mission to Asia, the proposal's being a precipitating factor leading to a major foreign missions enterprise. The first missionaries included Adoniram Judson and Luther Rice.[15]

Beyond the colleges, revival began in Northington, Connecticut, with meetings initiated by young people. Bennett Tyler was a sophomore at Yale in 1802 and powerfully impressed by the revival there. He later gathered twenty-five accounts of revival by pastors in New England. In those accounts, no less than twenty emphasized the role of youth in the movements. Revivals on college campuses have continued until today.[16]

Prayer Revival

The Prayer Revival of 1857–1858 was characterized by its wide appeal. Several colleges experienced revival during this time; J. Edwin Orr documenting revival movements at Oberlin, Yale, Dartmouth, Middlebury, Williams, Amherst, Princeton, and Baylor.[17] One pivotal feature of this revival in relation to young people was the bearing it had on twenty-year-old Dwight Lyman Moody. In 1857 Moody wrote of his impression of what was occurring in Chicago: "There is a great revival of religion in this city. . . . [It] seems as if God were here himself."[18] Biographer John Pollock wrote that "the revival of early 1857 tossed Moody out of his complacent view of religion."[19] Moody went on to make a marked impact for Christ during the rest of the nineteenth century.

An aspect of Moody's influence in regard to students that cannot be overlooked was his leadership in the Student Volunteer Movement. Although this movement's roots have been traced ultimately to the Second Great Awakening and the Haystack Meeting of 1806, it was Moody who in 1886 invited 251 students in Mount Hermon, Massachusetts, for a conference. As a result of these meetings, which were highlighted by A. T. Pierson's challenging address, one hundred students volunteered for overseas missions. In 1888 the Student Volunteer Movement was formally organized, with John R. Mott named chairman. Over the next several decades literally thousands of students went to serve as foreign missionaries.

The Twentieth Century

At the turn of the twentieth century, fresh winds of the Spirit again created new movements. These include the Welsh Revival—as well as other developments in the United States and abroad—the birth of modern-day Pentecostalism in 1901 and the subsequent Azusa Street revival. It's interesting to note Charles Parham's influence: one of the key occurrences in the outbreak of Pentecostalism involved students at a Bible school that Charles Parham began in Topeka, Kansas, in 1900; W. J. Seymour, the black pastor who was the catalyst for the Azusa Street revival in Los Angeles, was influenced greatly in 1905 at another Bible school in Houston set up by Parham.

The Welsh Revival concerns specifically the movement that began in 1904 in the tiny country of Wales. A key place of origin of that movement was a church in New Quay, Cardiganshire, where Joseph Jenkins was pastor. During a service, Jenkins asked for personal testimony in response to the question, "What does Jesus mean to you?" A young person, fifteen-year-old Florrie Evans, only recently converted, rose and said, "If no one else will, then I must say that I love the Lord Jesus with all my heart."

Her simple testimony caused many to begin openly surrendering all to Christ, and the fires of revival burned. The revival spread as young people went from church to church, testifying. Itinerant preacher Seth Joshua came to New Quay to speak and was powerfully impressed by the power of God evident there. He then journeyed to speak at Newcastle Embyn College, and the next week he spoke at nearby Blaenannerch.

A young coal miner named Evan Roberts, who was a ministerial student at Blaenannerch, experienced a powerful personal revival. He felt convicted to return to his home church to address the youth there. Seventeen heard him following a Monday service, he continued preaching, and revival began there.

The revival spread across the country, and news of the awakening spread worldwide. Colleges reported revival, including Denison University in Ohio. Incidentally, it was during this period that Southwestern Baptist Theological Seminary was born.

Throughout the twentieth century college campuses were a furnace for the flames of revival among youth. From Wheaton to Bethel to Asbury colleges, revival and students seemed to result in a spiritual chemical reaction, blessed in the laboratory of a sovereign God. Is your youth ministry, as it's practiced now, ready for the same chemistry? Is your church willing to be the next laboratory for revival? Are you ready to help it happen?

Chapter Six

The Jesus Movement

A Double-edged Sword

*Now when they saw the boldness of Peter and John, and
perceived that they were uneducated and untrained men,
they marveled. And they realized that they had been with
Jesus.*

—Acts 4:13

The year 1970 stands as a watershed. The Vietnam War protests were
at their height; Woodstock had taken place the year before, touching off the new impact of rock music; the country was in the heat of the
civil rights movement. In the church, 1970 witnessed the birth of Evangelism Explosion. That year is often cited as the beginning of the modern megachurch movement. And 1970 was a special year for me because
I met the Lord.

Imagine a skinny little boy, age eleven, with ears like Dumbo's and
the physique of a pipe cleaner. I felt like a zero with the outline erased, a
balloon with the skin peeled off, a nothing. On top of that, my folks had
named me Alvin—not exactly a manly name! (I love the name now; it's
not a boring name!) I was so insecure, I thought that God didn't like me
since I was so pathetic.

Then I saw God move. I watched Him take a bunch of hippie freaks
at our little church and turn them into Jesus freaks. Two guys from our
church were so excited about Jesus, they went to downtown Birmingham, Alabama, where I was born. There, they took the One Way street
signs and turned them straight up, pointing to heaven, all over part of
Birmingham. The pastor had to discipline them. He said, "Don't do
that." (That's not *evangelism,* that's *evandalism.*)

I had no idea our church was part of a larger phenomenon called the Jesus Movement. I just knew that if God could change a bunch of hippies like that, He could also use me. So that summer I gave my life to Jesus. And guess what? I have *never* recovered.

The Jesus Movement of the late 1960s and early 1970s touched a significant number of Baby Boomers. Hippies turned to Christ and baptized their music, resulting in the revolution known as contemporary Christian music (CCM); college revivals took hold in places like Asbury in 1970; through youth musicals *(Good News, Tell It Like It Is, Celebrate Life)*, and Explo '72 in Dallas, Texas, churches began to see more young faces; seminaries witnessed a huge influx of students. The Jesus Movement touched a generation of evangelicals. Today, many leaders among various denominational and parachurch groups are at some level products of the Jesus Movement. Examples include:

- hundreds, even thousands, of youth choir tours on mission across America singing *Good News, Celebrate Life*, or a similar score;
- drug-laced teens in California and elsewhere taking the eternal trip offered in the gospel;
- churches strengthened: in the Southern Baptist Convention alone, baptisms surpassed 400,000 for five years in a row, the only time this has ever happened (and the biggest percentage of youth baptisms ever);
- a generation of believers touched by the Spirit of God, many of whom now are leading the cry for revival in our time;
- the rise of CCM and the development of praise and worship music in churches;
- an explosion of megachurches, many of which can be directly traced to the Jesus Movement;
- perhaps most significant, a zealous commitment by multitudes of youth to share Christ one on one.

A Youth-Centered Revival

The Jesus Movement touched the youth population almost exclusively, especially appealing to young people outside the established church.

While the Jesus Movement is best known for the street Christians who teemed the coastal cities of California in the late 1960s and early 1970s, they were only part of a larger movement of the Spirit. Traditional churches, parachurch groups, and evangelical schools were also touched by the Jesus Movement.

The nonestablishment Jesus People were the most recognizable persons involved in the movement. "Jesus Freaks," *Time* magazine called them—"Evangelical hippies." Or, as many prefer to be called, "street Christians." Duane Pederson coined the terms *Jesus People* and *Jesus Movement,*[1] but "under different names . . . they are the latest incarnation of that oldest of Christian phenomena: footloose, passionate bearers of the Word."[2]

The Jesus Movement, though, spread beyond the Jesus Freaks who came out of the hippie or drug scene. "In associating the Jesus Movement with such a narrow group," Knight argued, "one misses the national pattern of the religious phenomena, which [touched] in one way or another most of the youth of the nation, those still at home, in school and out."[3]

Pederson agreed: "Though the Movement started as a ministry to the street people, it is much wider than that now. It is reaching the campuses—both high school and college. And it's definitely ministering to the youth of the establishment churches."[4]

More traditional expressions of Christianity were also affected by unique features of the Jesus Movement. Christian coffeehouses developed around the country as the Jesus Movement spread. "At the beginning," Jorstad observed, "each [coffeehouse] leader would generally follow the same pattern: rent a store in the inner city; turn it into a counseling center and coffeehouse with free sandwiches, coffee, and Kool Aid; and invite anyone interested to come in."[5]

Arthur Blessitt founded His Place in southern California, which ministered primarily to drug users, runaways, and similar individuals. First Baptist, Lake Jackson, Texas, sponsored The Anchor, a coffeehouse ministry on the Gulf coast. Hundreds of coffeehouses soon spread across the country, including The Fisherman's Net in Detroit, Michigan; Agape in Columbus, Ohio; and Powerhouse in Las Vegas.[6]

Evenings in the coffeehouses centered on Bible discussions, gospel rock music of some form, and, in many ways, a revival meeting. These houses differed from other rescue missions because they especially sought to reach young street people, and because of their lack of ties with other churches or agencies. My own church started a coffeehouse called the One Way Christian Night Club. Many coffeehouses eventually became churches.

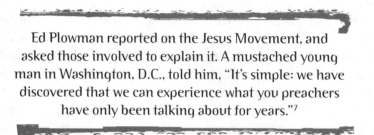

Ed Plowman reported on the Jesus Movement, and asked those involved to explain it. A mustached young man in Washington, D.C., told him, "It's simple: we have discovered that we can experience what you preachers have only been talking about for years."[7]

Some Jesus People began to live together in houses. Such communes had colorful names like Solid Rock House and Rejoice Always. They were generally characterized by a minimum of organization and high standards of morality and discipline.

Marches for Jesus, not unlike civil rights and other marches, began occurring around the nation. McFadden cited one march in New Orleans where "young longhairs with trumpets and drums have paraded up and down Bourbon Street imitating the traditional funeral procession in a demonstration of their faith."[8] In Fort Worth, Texas, over 13,500 youth marched down Main Street as a part of the Texas Baptist Youth Evangelism Conference, carrying signs that said things like "Turn on to Jesus," "Jesus Is Real." The chief of police in Fort Worth called it "one of the best things he'd seen in years, 'As American as ham and eggs.'"[9]

Festivals—large gatherings of people with music, testimonies, and speakers—emerged at about the same time as Woodstock. During the early years of the festivals and coffeehouses, CCM as a genre appeared. Jesus rock concerts developed as the movement progressed. The first big festival was the Faith Festival in Evansville, Indiana, March 27–28, 1970. Pat Boone and several folk-rock Christian groups were the featured leaders of the festival, and the musical *Tell It Like It Is* was presented by the Indianapolis Youth for Christ musical troupe. In 1971 a Faithfest drew fifteen thousand, and on March 9, 1971, the first of a series of rallies in Chicago drew nine thousand. The state Baptist Student Union Convention in Arkansas hosted a Jesus festival as part of the meeting in 1972.[10] Many festivals continue to the present time, with tens of thousands in attendance annually.

Unique baptismal services also characterized the movement. Don Matison baptized almost fifty new converts in an irrigation ditch after an evangelistic meeting in Enslen Park, Modesto, California. Denny Flanders, who led the Jesus Movement ministry called Maranatha, was featured on the front page of the *Washington Daily News* with a photograph of a baptismal ceremony in the Reflecting Pool at the Lincoln Memorial. Mass baptisms were well known. The *Indiana Baptist* reported the baptism of about one thousand young people by Chuck Smith of Calvary Chapel, Costa Mesa, California. Jess Moody said the first ocean baptisms were performed by Fenton Moorehead, associate at First Baptist, West Palm Beach, where Moody was pastor.[11]

The Jesus Movement in the Evangelical Church

In terms of theology, the movement was, in general, within the framework of conservative evangelicalism, although charismatic Christianity dominated in many segments. An article in *Newsweek* emphasized the movement's theological correlation to traditional Christianity: "In truth . . . many of the evangelists who have attached themselves to the Jesus Movement preach the same law-and-order message to the young that [Billy] Graham directs to the kids' parents. 'I really dig Graham,' says Rich Weaver, 25. 'He's a pretty far-out guy.'"[12]

Two of the clearest examples of the Jesus Movement's relation to evangelicalism in general were the simultaneous occurrences of the Asbury Revival[13] and the rapid rise of Campus Crusade for Christ, International. In 1970 Asbury College experienced a powerful revival that not only affected the college there but also spread to many other campuses. Campus Crusade rode the impetus of the Jesus Movement with its Explo '72 event in Dallas, Texas. Over eighty thousand young people attended the weeklong training sessions, which focused on winning the world to Christ within a generation. The Saturday following the event a day-long Christian music festival drew crowds estimated at 150,000 to 180,000. Billy Graham, one of the speakers at Explo, called it a Christian Woodstock.

Any historic movement, particularly one where God's hand has been at work, provides a laboratory for the contemporary church to discover how biblical principles are worked out in the context of a given cultural setting. The Jesus Movement offers principles that stand beyond the One Way signs, the psychedelic T-shirts, and the coffeehouses. What, then, can the Jesus Movement contribute to contemporary youth ministry?

The Jesus Movement was just that—a movement about Jesus. It began neither as a result of strategic planning by a think tank nor as a result of human effort. In today's youth ministry, obsessed with discovery of new trends, methods, and strategies, we'd be well advised to recall that many of the most effective methods and strategies to reach the world—whether it be missions, evangelism, or specifically church growth—have been born from times of awakening.[14] The latest technology and research may be of some help but, when it comes to youth ministry, God must be the source of anything eternal. In times of mighty revival, God simply pours out His Spirit on our land and, as in the Jesus Movement, young people joined God's work.

Jesus Movement's Effect on Church Life

In his retrospective, Walker Knight noted the rise of "super churches" following the Jesus Movement: "Twenty years ago only two or three congregations numbered near the 10,000-member mark. Today many cities can point to one or more super churches."[15]

Calvary Chapel in Costa Mesa, California, in the minds of many the mother church of the Jesus Movement, continues to be an example of the megachurch phenomenon. Beginning in 1965 with only twenty-five people, the church now has multiple thousands in attendance every week, and still practices mass baptisms in the ocean.

Calvary Chapel can be said to have produced offspring as well. Numerous congregations across America began with pastors who converted to Christianity at Calvary Chapel. Scores of young men in the Jesus Movement who attended Calvary Chapel and entered the ministry now lead large churches.

One of the most recognized examples is the Horizon Christian Fellowship in San Diego. Horizon began with twelve people, and now has 6,500 worshipers each Sunday, making it one of the largest churches in California. In addition, Horizon has started over thirty other churches. The church was founded by Mike MacIntosh, who in the late 1960s was a drug addict. He once turned himself in to the police as the "fifth Beatle." One night in 1970, MacIntosh attended Calvary Chapel. Chuck Girard and his group, Love Song, sang that night, followed by a message from Lonnie Frisbee, one of the earliest leaders of the Jesus Movement. MacIntosh committed his life to Jesus Christ, and in 1971—after moving into the communal house, Mansion Messiah—he and his former wife were remarried.[16] Of particular interest, before founding Horizon, MacIntosh was director of Maranatha Music, a CCM company beginning out of Calvary Chapel.

Greg Laurie, another Calvary Chapel alumni, has become one of the better known evangelists of the present day. Laurie also pastors Harvest Christian Fellowship in Riverside, California, with well over twelve thousand members. Converted at Calvary Chapel, Laurie began Harvest Fellowship in 1972 as a Bible study, and now speaks at Billy Graham-sized crusades. A 1991 citywide meeting in Anaheim had a total of 200,000 in attendance. At the final service 51,000 attended, the largest crowd in that stadium for such a meeting since Graham had been there ten years prior.[17]

Another example of a megachurch that resulted from the Jesus Movement is Elmbrook Church in Milwaukee, which grew at a tremendous rate (350 to two thousand) from 1970–1972. The church, in fact, had to relocate more than once because of its rapid growth. To a great extent the large influx of young people caused the church to reorganize, Pastor Stuart Briscoe initiating small-group ministries to aid in the integration of large numbers.[18]

Even the much-studied Willow Creek Community Church near Chicago, Illinois, can trace its roots in no small measure to the Jesus Movement. Willow Creek had its origin in 1972 with Bill Hybels and a few friends. They had formed the Son Company, a band that played "high voltage Christian rock music."[19] Hybels and friend Dave Holmbo founded Son City, a youth ministry that soon grew to more than one thousand young people. The leaders sought new approaches:

They looked for contemporary methods to spread the age-old truth that Jesus saves. It was risky business. They tossed away the clichés and brought in the electric guitars. "The thing you have to remember," says associate pastor Don Cousins, another original member of Son City, "is that what we were doing was totally radical, even sacrilegious to a lot of people." . . . At that time, there were no contemporary Christian music stations.[20]

Hybels, as well as others, recognized the time was right for radical changes in ministry. He observed, "It was the time of the Jesus People and One Way bumper stickers." Thousands were reached through his ministry, and Willow Creek ultimately was born. Each weekend Willow Creek has over fifteen thousand in attendance, making it, according to some analysts, the church having the largest number in attendance in the United States.

Many Southern Baptist churches, too, became megachurches in the early 1970s. Houston's First Baptist exploded following the arrival of Pastor John Bisagno, who was both aware of and open to the Jesus Movement. During the same period, Rehoboth Baptist Church was one of Georgia's fastest-growing. Knight observed, "Such super churches as Rehoboth appear to be a legacy of the Jesus Movement and its influence."[21]

In examining the rise of the megachurch, one cannot overlook the vitality, the passion, and the commitment of youth. How much research has been done, though, regarding the impact of youth on growing churches? In my own travels, I've spoken in almost eight hundred churches. Of those that did *not* have an outstanding youth presence, only a handful were vibrant, evangelistic, and growing.

The Jesus Movement's Effect on Worship Music

The most enduring impact of the Jesus Movement is its influence on music and worship style. Because of the importance of music in general in youth culture, the role of music in the youth-initiated Jesus Movement was crucial.

In the 1970s most musicians in the Jesus Movement had been so radically saved they simply sang out of gratitude for Christ. Larry Norman was one of the best-known leaders of Jesus Movement music. His simple ballad about the second coming of Christ, "I Wish We'd All Been Ready," was a signature song of the movement. Chuck Girard and his group, Love Song, were referred to by some as the "Beatles of the Christian music world." Nancy Honeytree converted to Christianity in 1970 and soon began to sing a blend of pop and folk music in many coffeehouses and churches. Billy Ray Hearn, one of the early leaders in the development of youth musicals, later became an executive with Sparrow Records and offered Honeytree her first contract. Don Francisco, son of Southern Baptist Theological Seminary professor Clyde Francisco, was a familiar artist in the early years. Annie Herring became a Christian in 1968 and began singing in California. With her sister, Nelly, and brother, Matthew, she formed a group known as the Second Chapter of Acts, a group that remained very popular until they disbanded in 1988.

Barry McGuire epitomizes the rock singer-turned-contemporary Christian artist. In 1965, McGuire's protest song "Eve of Destruction" was one of the biggest hits in rock music. McGuire later had a lead role in the Broadway musical *Hair,* which was not exactly the centerpiece of evangelicalism! Then in 1970, McGuire picked up a *Good News for Modern Man* translation of the New Testament. As a result, he committed his life to Christ, and traded rock music for the music of the Jesus Movement.

Keith Green sang about radical obedience. In 1972 Eddie DeGarmo and Dana Key formed one of the most enduring duos in contemporary Christian music's young history. They were already playing rock music when they began openly singing Christian lyrics. At the time, they knew nothing of Larry Norman or any other Jesus Movement music.

So, then, CCM had its birth in the Jesus Movement, and CCM's role in changing the face of church music can't be denied. Yet it can be argued that the most important impact of Jesus Movement music is not the rise of CCM but the blossoming of praise and worship music. The words and melodies of this new music that honors God is taking a generation of people—mostly young but also old—to new levels of worship.

Evangelism

The Jesus Movement emphasized the biblical truth that the church is a hospital for sinners, not a hotel for saints. It was thus evangelistic to the core—hence the focus on Jesus. "One way," the cry of the Jesus Movement devotees, emphasized the need for all to come to salvation through Jesus. Some of the hippie converts in the 1970s had more confidence in the exclusivity of the cross than some so-called evangelical writers of the time.[22]

The Jesus Movement demonstrated that youth can and will embrace truth. Although youth in the 1970s were confronted with Eastern mysticism and the rise of New Age metaphysics, they still turned to Jesus. Today youth are confronted with neo-paganism (like Wicca) and vague forms of spiritism. Should we learn from history? Or should we cave in to postmodern relativism? Jesus is still the only way.

Problems Created by the Jesus Movement

Anything with the potential for good also has the potential for harm. The Jesus Movement featured passionate young zealots but they were, for the most part, outside the mainstream of church life. For all the good brought about by the Jesus Movement, it also sowed seeds that produced some negative long-term effects.

The Need for Doctrine

The emphasis of the Jesus Movement was on simple faith and a personal relationship with Jesus. But one of the greatest weaknesses of the Jesus Movement was its theological superficiality. This resulted from two main factors. First, it was fundamentally a youth movement, so it lacked the maturity of theological reflection. Second, it was overall anti-institutional, keeping it from accountability provided by the church.

The failure of the Jesus Movement to become incorporated into the institutional church lies partly with those involved in the movement itself. While many within the movement cautioned about the dangers of anti-church sentiments, emotionalism, and so forth, others failed to recognize the significance of the local church.

On the other hand, much of the blame lies with local churches. Many churches were appreciative of the young Christians, particularly those coming off the streets. Various church leaders were, in fact, emphatic on the importance of churches incorporating the movement. Richard Hogue stated this clearly: "If we don't discipline these kids—if the Jesus Movement folds, it will be the church's responsibility."[23] This attitude of inclusion was, however, by no means the rule. Many churches refused to open their doors to many of the youth, particularly those out of the counterculture, and many Southern Baptists as well as other traditions were opposed virtually *in toto* to the Jesus Movement.

One result of this exclusion was the birth of various sectarian movements. The Children of God cult arose from the period, as well as many independent, nondenominational churches, ranging theologically from evangelical to heretical. If nothing else, the Jesus Movement provides a valuable lesson for churches and denominations in general. We must guard against defining spirituality in such a way that when a movement does not meet the definition, it is ignored or even resisted. Also, when deviations occur within a movement, the response should not be to disqualify the entire movement based on some extremes.[24] That's not to say that any movement should be accepted uncritically; however, history is full of believers who, in their day, resisted what was later seen as a movement of God.

The Increase of Segregation in Youth Ministry

The Jesus Movement has been criticized, and rightfully so, because it was driven more by emotion than by doctrine. That critique further supports the concern that we have failed to adequately equip young people in theology: how much greater might the Jesus Movement have been if the many zealous youth had been given proper guidance?

Not that the church utterly failed to try. With the explosion of megachurches that grew out of the Jesus Movement came the need for effective ministers to deal with various groups within the church. Thus, the Jesus Movement helped to precipitate the rise of full-time youth ministers. It wasn't long before youth ministry became segregated from the mainstream of the church. Today, one can be an active teen member in many churches and, except for the Sunday morning service, never be around anyone except other teens and a handful of adult "youth workers."

The practical result of this student-ministry subculture has not been
to create a generation of spiritual giants in the youth population. Rather,
students in the church are being treated with less respect, further rein-
forcing the theory of adolescence described earlier. So in spite of its evidence of God at work in the lives of youth, the Jesus Movement, by
virtue of its adherents and its music, helped to foster a segregated approach to youth. That approach worked in the long term to separate
youth from adults in the church.

Nevertheless, God touched a generation who did much for the kingdom. Should God touch the Millennial generation with a fresh wind of
revival, will we embrace it or oppose it? What if God begins a work
among the most unchurched segment of the youth culture? Many
churches missed seeing the hand of God upon youth in the Jesus Movement because those churches focused too much on the long hair and
strange clothing. Could we today miss seeing God at work because we're
too busy planning activities for youth rather than actively planning how
to reap the potential of youth?

PART 2

Reinventing Youth Ministry

Dr. Reid,

Here's a lesson I taught myself—and I taught it to my-self when I was running our four-mile run at soccer try-outs, so it kind of relates to both. Okay—I figure that being a Christian is like being a soccer player running for tryouts (like me), and once you first start running or first become a Christian, things are okay. Then sooner or later you find things—like lungs in my case—or people who will let you down in life. And you get discouraged and once you get discouraged enough you want to stop or quit or start walking. So I walked. And walking is kind of like pulling away from God or not being on fire anymore. Then someone comes catching up to you or even pulling back to help you. And they give you the encouragement that you need (in this case I got encouragement from my team-mates), and once you get that encouragement the things that let you down before (even lungs) don't seem to matter any-more—like they outweigh it. And you're back on track running again and wanting to sprint and run faster (like growing in the Lord). I think when you came to our church most of us were walking, and then your encouragement and your love for Jesus wanted to make us run and catch up. I don't know if you get it. I kind of confuse myself sometimes, but I just thought I'd share. I've got to get to school now. Talk to you later.

Miranda

In her own way, Miranda describes the vital role older adults can have in the lives of young adults. We who work with, live with, and love youth have an opportunity—more than that, a responsibility—to en-courage youth.

Years ago a friend of mine wrote an article about spiritual "anesthe-tists." Anesthetists are people in the church who, through various means, dull believers' responses to radical Christianity. Those who would anes-thetize the church from raising the bar for teens say things like

- "We don't want *those* kinds of kids in our church";
- "All those youth do is mess up the church";
- "They're young, so don't push them too hard";
- "I want to know why you don't focus more on *my* kids."

These kinds of attitudes from adults in the church, as well as the Pied Piper mentality of some youth pastors, are part of the reason we're not developing the potential of youth. It's time to cross the line in the sand. It's time to listen to God, not to people. It's time to raise the bar. In particular, we must raise the bar for youth in vital areas: prayer, Bible knowledge, evangelism, and worship. Further, we must set a new stan-dard for parents and the local church. How? Read on.

Chapter Seven

Life Is Short. Pray Hard

So when they heard that, they raised their voice to God with one accord and said: "Lord, You are God, who made heaven and earth and the sea, and all that is in them, who by the mouth of Your servant David have said:

> *'Why did the nations rage,*
> *And the people plot vain things?*
> *The kings of the earth took their stand,*
> *And the rulers were gathered together*
> *Against the Lord and against His Christ.'*

"For truly against Your holy Servant Jesus, whom You anointed, both Herod and Pontius Pilate, with the Gentiles and the people of Israel, were gathered together to do whatever Your hand and Your purpose determined before to be done. Now, Lord, look on their threats, and grant to Your servants that with all boldness they may speak Your word, by stretching out Your hand to heal, and that signs and wonders may be done through the name of Your holy Servant Jesus."

And when they had prayed, the place where they were assembled together was shaken; and they were all filled with the Holy Spirit, and they spoke the word of God with boldness.

—Acts 4:24–31

When I was a sophomore in high school, an older youth gave me a booklet that profoundly changed me. This particular booklet, produced by Campus Crusade for Christ, was called a "transferable concept," that is, a concept easily transferred from one person to another. The subject of this booklet was prayer. Never before had I seen anything like this. Never before had I been so encouraged and instructed to pray.

That little booklet was the beginning of my journey to pursue intimacy with God. At age fifteen, I was ready to learn in the school of prayer, but had that older youth not given me that booklet, I would've missed the opportunity. From that day until now I've been consumed with the desire to see a great movement of God and to help others enroll in the school of prayer.

A central focus of raising up a generation to impact the culture should start with teaching them and showing them how to know God. In a given week at your church, how many hours do the youth spend together as a group? Include Sunday school, youth Bible study, a Wednesday night youth service, or anything your church does. Of those hours, how much time is spent in prayer? When students finish high school and leave your youth ministry, what do they believe about prayer, and how do they practice prayer?

Lest you think youth have no interest in prayer, consider See You at the Pole, an annual event each September where millions of youth meet to pray around flagpoles at schools. In September 2000, approximately three million students gathered at their schools' flagpoles for the seventh annual See You at the Pole prayer event, marking perhaps the largest simultaneous prayer meeting in American history. See You at the Pole has sparked a nationwide interest in prayer among teens.[1]

While See You at the Pole is the most visible example of youth at prayer, it is far from the only one. In September 2000, I spoke at a church just west of Asheville, North Carolina. That afternoon I went out witnessing with some church members. One of them commented that she had gone to a "We Still Pray" rally in Asheville just weeks before. "Well," she said, "I never made it to the rally. Three of us sat in traffic, but one person I know made it in." Little wonder that there was a traffic jam. One newspaper estimated that 35,000 came to the rally on August 17 to protest the Supreme Court's ruling that June about school prayer at ball games. As a result, "We Still Pray" rallies have sprung up across the nation. Christians have been encouraged, and across America many have risen in a spontaneous recitation of the Lord's Prayer after the national anthem at ball games.[2]

An Awesome Way to Pray

"I consider myself one of the biggest supporters of See You at the Pole," says Barry St. Clair, founder of Reach Out Ministries, a youth ministry training organization in Atlanta. "But I wondered, *How can we take this thing from a one-day event to a national movement among our young people?*" Pursuing this question with much prayer and diligent effort, Reach Out Ministries developed the Pole2Locker concept, now called "An Awesome Way to Pray."

An Awesome Way to Pray, says St. Clair, is "designed to help young people take their commitment for Christ, demonstrated at the See You at the Pole event, to their lockers—that is, to their spheres of influence in their schools." An Awesome Way to Pray is a six-week intensive training course designed to help today's teens reach their peers with the gospel. It focuses on three main things: loving friends, living the life, and telling the story. "When we as leaders demonstrate genuine concern for young people," says St. Clair, "and equip them to live out their faith, we energize them for the work of the kingdom. They are changed—and so are we."[3]

High school students in Modesto, California, are doing Jericho-style prayer walks around every school in their city. Mike Higgs reported in *Pray!* Magazine that in places like Littleton, Colorado, students began establishing prayer groups on every campus in their community. It is of special interest that Higgs' article highlighted Littleton, Colorado, in an issue that was published just months *before* the shootings at Columbine. He noted that there was a vision for seeing campus prayer groups established throughout metropolitan Denver and across the nation. Young people from Portland, Oregon, to Buffalo, New York, are engaging in protracted times of united prayer, literally crying out to God for their peers, schools, and communities.[4] Higgs commented:

There seems to be an unprecedented, unplanned, unusual, and unstoppable explosion of prayer among youth! It's unprecedented, at least in modern times, because of the sheer number of participants. It's unplanned because it's not the result of some new youth ministry program or activity. It appears to be a quite spontaneous work of the Holy Spirit, and nobody is trying to control it. It's unusual because such passion for prayer is not what's expected from a postmodern, relativistic, diversity-embracing culture. And it's unstoppable because it can't be legislated out of the schools—you can take prayer out of schools, but you can't take the praying students out![5]

Recent articles in *Time* magazine, the *Washington Post*, and other publications, as well as a special report on CNN, have brought national attention to this grassroots movement. Further attention was focused after the shooting in Paducah, Kentucky—the victims were in a school prayer group. But media publicity only touches the tip of the iceberg. During a series of national youth leader meetings that surrounded the National Day of Prayer gathering in Washington, D.C., testimony after testimony circulated through the groups about how God is stirring up prayer in youth.

And how critical a time it is to teach and challenge youth to pray. More and more, phrases such as *moral wilderness* and *desert wasteland* are being used to describe our cultural terrain. Some people borrow the biblical terms *dry bones* and *desolation* to note the increasing depravity, the loss of personal integrity, and the idolatry of our time. Many point to the absence even within the church of a distinctively Christian character.

But as we survey today's society, some signs of hope and new life can be spotted on the horizon—in the vibrancy and passion of Christian youth. These praying young people may be the precursors to one of the greatest movements of God's Spirit we've seen.

Beginning in January of 1995, God's Spirit moved in a powerful revival in Brownwood, Texas. From there, it spread to other churches and some college campuses. I was blessed to be at some churches where God's hand moved powerfully. Some services lasted for hours, resulting in many conversions, families being restored, and lives being changed. I saw young people set free from pornography, eating disorders, and other maladies. Prayer played a huge role in the genesis of that movement—students at

Howard Payne University and Coggin Avenue Baptist Church had prayed for months prior to the revival's onset. A student named Tim at Howard Payne testified about the spontaneous prayer that began on his campus prior to a movement of revival beginning February 1995:

> As school began this spring, there was anticipation about what God was about to do with the students. Spontaneous prayer began on campus. About thirty or forty students . . . gathered on campus. They worshiped and praised the Lord. They called these meetings "Jesus parties." I was at one that went until 1:00 A.M. I thought it was strange that college students would give up Friday nights to worship God.[6]

When is the last time you challenged your students to set aside time to cry out to God for a movement worthy of His great name?

The Power of Prayer

Youth leader, consider—Do those you lead see you as a person of prayer? Do they see a hunger to know God? Parents, do your children recognize the fruit of your daily devotional life? Are they learning from your teaching and example how to walk with God? Are you praying God-sized prayers in the ministry of your church?

Revival is a lifestyle of obedience to God, and such a lifestyle is born out of a life of prayer. I define prayer this way: *intimacy with God that leads to the fulfillment of His purposes.* Intimacy is more than just talking. Prayer paves the road to a close, daily, personal walk with our Lord, which in turn leads to the fulfillment of His purposes. Although we may pray for the needs of ourselves and others, prayer is not merely a wish list for a Santa Claus-like benefactor; it's our way to learn God's purposes for us. Remember, life is not primarily about us but about Him.

One of the most foundational, practical, and real ways to prepare youth to change their world is through teaching them how daily to meet God. In most discussions of worship today, one infers that worship is primarily a corporate act that *can* be done privately. And such might be argued from the Old Testament, which is replete with public ceremonies.

But in the New Testament, worship is characterized as primarily a private act that can be done corporately. It's true that corporate worship plays an essential role in a believer's life (chap. 10 addresses that aspect of Christianity). But the strength of corporate worship grows out of the individual—and family—worship of believers during the week.[7]

Imagine Sunday at a typical church. Most come with an attitude something like this: "It's been a tough week, and I sure need my spiritual batteries recharged!" Certainly, Sunday worship should encourage and build up believers, but if we aren't careful we'll start to see church as the place that gives us our weekly "fix." A more accurate idea of worship is this: individual believers in church spend time daily with God in prayer, in His Word, seeking Him, and watching Him work daily. Families also pray together daily. Then individuals meet as a body on Sunday, not simply to get a "fix," but to give corporate expression to their individual worship. Now that would be a worship service!

How do you teach youth to begin that daily worship time? Start by observing your own daily worship time. Below are some practical tips to help you have a daily, close walk with God. But first let me assure you that prayer is not merely theoretical to me. As a young pastor I served a church with a checkered past and a declining enrollment. I was inexperienced, basically ignorance on fire! I made many mistakes, but I did one thing right: I taught the people to pray. I put together a seminar on how to have a daily prayer time, which helped many. Before an evangelistic meeting we held an all-night prayer session. I reasoned that if Jesus prayed all night before choosing His disciples, our pitiful church needed to pray even more. And God moved mightily—a church that had seen three people saved in eight years saw ten come to Christ in four days. But the foundation of that prayer session was laid when our people learned to pray daily.

> When faced with a busy day, save time by
> skipping your devotional time.
> —signed, the Devil

Here are some practical tips for prayer.

1. *Read the Bible.* As you set aside time daily, start by reading the Bible. If you don't know where to begin, try reading a chapter of Proverbs each day, reading a chapter that goes with the day of the month (Prov. 1 for May 1, for example).
2. *Keep a spiritual journal.* I've kept one for many years. Many of the spiritual giants in history—John Wesley, David Brainerd, George Whitefield, Jim Elliot—kept a journal. I like to write a little about the day before (I usually start out with "Yesterday I . . ."). Then, I share my requests, and sometimes my plans.
3. *Follow a pattern.* Jesus offered us a pattern for prayer in the model prayer found in Matthew 6. This prayer, also called the Lord's Prayer, is not a formula to repeat but a model to emulate. Notice these features that can help guide our praying:

- *God is close:* "Our Father . . ." We can know God intimately through Christ. *Begin by acknowledging the wonder of salvation* that allows us to speak to the Creator of the universe with such a personal term as "Father."
- *God is far:* "Who is in heaven . . ." God is not the "man upstairs." We can approach Him intimately as Father, yet with deep reverence as the great God who lives in a "high and lofty place" (Isa. 57:15). *Take time to reflect on His greatness.*
- *God is holy:* "Hallowed be Your name . . ." The essential attribute of God is holiness. Throughout the Bible the threefold cry toward God is never "love, love, love," or "judge, judge, judge," but "holy, holy, holy." This reminds us of both the uniqueness of our God and the depravity of our sin. *Allow the Spirit to show you any unconfessed sin or unresolved issues, and bring them to God in confession and repentance.*
- *God is redeemer:* "Your kingdom come, Your will be done . . ." How is the kingdom of God established? Through the gift of eternal life in Christ. So this prayer includes a focus on evangelism, for when we pray for the kingdom to come, we pray for all to be a part of God's family; when we pray for His will to be done, we're reminded that it's not God's will that any perish, but that all come to know

Him (see 2 Peter 3:9). *Take time to pray for lost people, that the kingdom of God would become theirs through salvation.*

- *God is provider:* "Give us this day . . ." While the kingdom comes before other needs, God is concerned for our lives. *We can pray for the temporal, physical, and emotional needs of ourselves and others. In fact, we must!*
- *God is merciful:* "Forgive us . . ." *Here we can pray for both our own sins and our willingness to forgive others.* If we daily take time to confess and forsake our own sin, and in that light to forgive those who hurt us, life will be much better.
- *God is our guide:* "And lead us not . . ." *Pray for direction in decisions, not toward evil, but toward Him.*
- *God is worthy of praise:* "For thine . . ." *Beginning our prayer time with a focus on God, and ending with praise, makes the time of prayer a blessing indeed.*

Another simple way to help a young believer learn to pray is by suggesting and following the little guide ACTS:

- *A is for Adoration.* Spend some time praising God for His greatness. You might listen to a praise and worship song as part of this time, or read a psalm of praise like Psalm 100 or 150.
- *C is for Confession.* Ask God to reveal any sins and confess them (1 John 1:9). Reading the Bible sometimes helps to reveal a sin that you need to address.
- *T is for Thanksgiving.* Growing Christians are grateful Christians. Thank God for salvation and for His specific blessings.
- *S is for Supplication.* This is a big word meaning to ask God for your needs and for the needs of others. How do you know God answers if you aren't praying specifically? I like to keep a list of specific things for which I am praying. Then, when God answers, I write that down, which really encourages me. As a junior in high school I began to pray specifically for the lady I would marry one day. I would never have had the honor of meeting and marrying Michelle without prayer. God does answer.

Here are a few practical things you can do to help maintain a daily devotional time:

1. *Make your devotional time a priority.* I'm sure you have a busy life—we all do. But you make time to do what you believe to be important. Set aside a time to spend with God, and stick to it as much as possible. Remember, sometimes you won't feel like praying, but you should pray because it's right, not because of your emotions.

2. *Designate a set time and place for your time with God.* Guard the time. For me it's first thing in the morning. Find a time best for you. If you don't have a time set aside daily to spend with Jesus, think about this: you take time daily to eat, to sleep, and (I hope) to clean up. Surely God is worth some of our time as well. Give up a ridiculous TV show for Jesus. As a Christian, you'll never mature further than the time you spend with God.

3. *Do whatever is necessary to be spiritually prepared.* Take a shower, listen to a song, or turn on some lights. I need a fresh cup of coffee.

4. *Occasionally adjust the elements of your devotional time to avoid monotony.* Sometimes I pray first, then read God's Word; sometimes I reverse that, and so on.

5. *As you pray, make the Scriptures a part of your time.* A great saint of prayer from years ago said, "We can do more than pray after we pray, but we cannot do more than pray until we pray."[8]

6. *Keep a journal.*[9]

This Generation Holds the Key

Youth are capable of discovering the basis of a revived life. Those students who are on the road of revival are there not because of wishful thinking or emotional exuberance. They're there because they know they've been purchased, rescued, and ransomed by a gracious God. This knowledge leads to gratitude, worship, and true inner joy. Most young people, when they choose to confess their sin and devote themselves to Christ, become keenly aware of the ravages of sin in their lives and in our culture. It's against this backdrop that God seems to be moving teen-agers into a new frontier. In virtually every region of the country, revival passion among young people has formed a spring that is slowly but surely trickling into the cultural desert.

Youth are capable, too, of knowing that God can use them mightily. As established in part 1 of this book, God has a heart for the young. Biblical history, as well as church history, reveals that when God moves in dramatic ways, young people are often at the center of the movement or are the ones most greatly affected. The traits of youthful believers should, then, give us hope—and perspective—for today and the future. Let us, then, allow God to use that passion, teaching our youth the power in a life of prayer.

As has also discussed in part 1, youth are taking an interest in spiri-tual matters. An example of this interest in spiritual growth among young people is reflected in Internet use. Barna notes that in 2001, 57 percent of the adult population made use of the Internet at home, work, or play. Among teenagers, however, 91 percent use the net. Teens also go online more than adults and stay online for longer periods of time. One Internet trend Barna discovered is the significant growth in the number of young people who use the Internet to maintain relationships. I know of many young people who, after school and homework spend their afternoons online, chatting with their peers. Barna discovered, too, an increase in the number of young people who are using the Net to help themselves spiritually—not in the Internet church, but to obtain a short religious devotional, or to submit prayer request, or things of that nature.[10]

Read Mark 1:35. Even the Lord Jesus spent much time in prayer. How much more do we need to spend time with God? If you ever get frustrated with prayer, maybe you need to remind yourself how God often works in prayer. When you ask God something,
  • sometimes God says no because the request is wrong (we sometimes ask for things that God knows will hurt us);
  • sometimes God says slow because the timing is

wrong (God is never early or late, but sometimes we are impatient);
- sometimes God says grow because we are wrong (sometimes we are just not spiritually mature enough yet);
- but when the request is right, and the time is right, and we are right, God says go.

A Word to Parents

Many complain that prayer today has been taken out of public schools. But how many of those who complain pray with their children in their homes? Lifeway Christian Resources informs us that 92 percent of Christian homes have no devotional time in an entire year!

This past Saturday my kids helped me plant a lot of grass seed at our house. That night, during our family devotional time, I asked Josh to pray for rain. He did, and immediately after that, it began to rain. Before Josh could put himself on the level of Elijah, his sister, Hannah, reminded him the next morning that he had also prayed for her to feel better, and she still felt sick.

Still, prayer matters, and young people should learn how to communicate with God personally while they are still children. Why? Our culture has robbed youth of their sense of wonder, of awe toward God. A way to keep a sense of wonder among youth comes through regular times of prayer.

The church itself has abetted in the robbery. Churches argue over worship style and such issues as whether or not to clap, while neglecting the weightier matters of substance and the presence of the Spirit. We as parents and leaders of youth can raise the bar of prayer for this generation, starting with our own walk with God. If we teach youth the central role of prayer, the impact on the church could be staggering.

Greg Stier utilizes a Prayer-Dare-Share Strategy of leading youth to witness. He starts with prayer, challenging students to pray weekly for their unsaved friends by name in a Sunday school or youth meeting. What, though, is the focus of prayer in most churches? As a professor of evangelism, on the first day of class I help students to see that 90 percent of requests are health-related. The Bible, of course, teaches us to pray for the sick. But what about praying for harvesters (Matt. 9:36–38)? What about praying for the kingdom of God to increase (Matt. 6), and remembering that it does so by the salvation of the lost? What about praying for lost friends, emulating the passion of Paul in Romans 10? We can pray for those who are sick physically, but how much more should we pray for those who are currently dead spiritually (Eph. 2)?

Such is the challenge Stier gives to youth. He adds,

> I am not talking [only] about casual prayer once a week. . . . I am talking about intense, intentional prayer every day. I am talking about kids making up top ten lists of their friends and family members and praying consistently both in and out of their youth groups for the people on those lists.[11]

My family is involved in a church that takes seriously the responsibility of praying for the lost. We have a 4 x 4 strategy that grows out of our mission statement: *find* those who need Jesus, *feed* all on the Word, until they are *fully* established in Christ. The "4 x 4" strategy involves

- 4 people—get to know 4 lost people you seek for the Lord
- 4 prayers—pray daily 4 times for their salvation
- 4 parties—we have at least 4 major evangelistic events, from a Halloween alternative to Easter musicals
- 4 Him

We named the strategy 4 x 4 because some people are so far from God we need a 4 x 4 to reach them!

The best strategy without prayer is like
the fastest car without gas.[12]

Five years from now the spiritual condition of your students will not be determined foremost by your programs or activities. It will not be gauged by your teaching on worship. No, the number one reason your students will be stronger spiritually five years from now is because they have learned to pray.

Chapter Eight

Teaching the Youth Well

Give ear, O my people, to my law;
Incline your ears to the words of my mouth.
I will open my mouth in a parable;
I will utter dark sayings of old,
Which we have heard and known,
And our fathers have told us.
We will not hide them from their children,
Telling to the generation to come the praises of the Lord,
And His strength and His wonderful works that He has done.

For He established a testimony in Jacob,
And appointed a law in Israel,
Which He commanded our fathers,
That they should make them known to their children;
That the generation to come might know them,
The children who would be born,
That they may arise and declare them to their children,
That they may set their hope in God,
And not forget the works of God,
But keep His commandments;
And may not be like their fathers,
A stubborn and rebellious generation,
A generation that did not set its heart aright,
And whose spirit was not faithful to God.

—Psalm 78:1–8 (emphasis added)

Dr. Reid:

The people at my church are so VERY far away from God, and I want to start a Bible study. It's so horrible at my church. . . . All of the people are older than me, and they are . . . complete snobs. . . . Last weekend, I took Rob to my youth group (I'm trying really hard to be more involved) and the people served us lunch. Rob and I sat down at this one table to eat, and this girl picked up her stuff and moved away because we sat down there. . . . That's typically what I go through. We went to Sunday school and Rob saw what it was like. They never even mentioned God, except for the few times Rob and I did. The conversations quickly died down though. I really want youth in my church to know God!

God bless you,
Pam

This is an edited e-mail from a youth who desperately wants to know God, but can't find Him in the people at her church. Her love for Jesus is, in fact, denigrated by the very people who should rejoice in it. Her name has been changed, but her story is real.

Youth crave spiritual reality: Note the growth of Wicca in the youth culture; the variety of shows on spiritual (not necessarily Christian) themes that appeal to youth. Check out the programming on the WB network, the most watched by youth, to see what I mean. It's a sad irony, then, that the youth who crave authentic spirituality are not being taught from the richest treasure of spirituality ever known—the Bible. What are we doing to open its wealth to students?

Every Generation Must Be Taught Anew

A funny thing happened to me on the way to the North Carolina Snake and Reptile Exhibit a couple of years ago. I love reptiles, but more about that later (in chap. 9). I somehow convinced my dean, Russ Bush, to go along with us—me, my elementary school-aged daughter, Hannah, and a couple of students.

In the midst of observing several thousand snakes, lizards, and other exotics, Russ and I were discussing young people in general and youth ministry in particular. "Alvin," Russ observed, "we have to teach every generation all over again. We cannot assume they know all they should about biblical truth."

His comment stopped me dead in my tracks like meeting a full-grown rattler on a lonely mountain trail. It was so simple, yet so profound. Every generation has a fresh opportunity to make an impact—but there's a real chance that every generation will miss the lessons from the past.

Second Chronicles 34 records the account of young King Josiah and his reforms. At age sixteen Josiah began to seek the Lord, and by age twenty he was leading a major reform. The key to the change for his generation was not innovation or technology. The key was the discovery of the Law. Read the account and just imagine—God's people had lost the Bible.

I'm afraid the Bible has been lost, too, in many youth ministries, and the result is too many Josiahs miss the chance to do great things for God. Certainly innovation and technology have their place. I'm a member of a contemporary, innovative church, and I've learned to fear neither the clear teachings of Scripture nor innovation. I've used PowerPoint and object lessons, and have even brought snakes into a service (as an object lesson, not to test one's faith). Still, I'd argue that the hope for the future of youth ministry must be based in *truth,* not *technique.* Before consulting the latest youth website or magazine, a good place for a youth pastor to start in raising the bar of Bible knowledge would be to read the entire Bible with an eye to its references to youth.

What can be more a important thing to give a young person than the truth of God's Word? And this truth must be communicated in a context that encourages long-term growth and maturation, that is, in the *church.* Richard R. Dunn makes the point well:

> A mature theological framework considers the implications of God's design of the local church not only as a place where children and youth participate in an intentional, intergenerational faith community.
>
> Guiding the ministry into the faith community is critical.

> Students' spiritual growth is stunted if they are lacking in spiri-
> tual relationships with peers *and* adults. Peers may have the most
> immediate impact on an adolescent. Parents and adult men-
> tors, however, have the most important long-term effect on stu-
> dents' lives. By God's design, students need to belong to and
> participate in the life of the local church.[1]

There's another reason we must teach biblical truth to young people.
This generation will not buy doctrine just because the church says it's
the truth. Bombarded by postmodern relativism on one side, and anemic churches on the other, students today must be shown both *what* to
believe and *why.* They must not only *hear* the truth; they must *experience*
it. Thus, in a pluralistic culture, apologetics will have an increasingly
vital role among Christian youth to help them build a strong personal
faith.

Biblical Truth Matters

Greg Stier is on track when he states that "within the pages of Scripture we have everything we need to truly be successful in youth ministry."[2] Most youth pastors would agree with that statement, but our
practice doesn't always match our theory. In defense of youth ministers,
part of the reason they neglect strong biblical teaching is that so many
never learned how to study the Scriptures themselves.

For whatever reason, though, too many youth leaders today have,
without even realizing it, minimized the role of the Word in their ministries. Certainly this isn't intentional, but it's too often reality. I recently
spoke to four hundred students at a megachurch. They were wired. But
only 10 percent brought their Bibles. If they don't need their Bibles at
church, why would they need them at home?

In November 2001, I presented a paper based upon the subject of
this book at the Evangelical Theological Society (ETS) annual meeting
in Colorado. Two professors of youth ministry attended the session,
during which I made the statement found in chapter 2: Too many youth
ministers learn youth ministry from youth ministers who learn it from
youth ministers. So the training they receive is essentially "monkey-see,

monkey-do," which is great for learning practical tips, but awful in terms of biblical reflection or evaluation of trends, movements, or methods. Further, most who have a seminary degree have taken few courses in Bible and none in the biblical languages. Thus, few youth ministers have either the background to teach the Word or the ability to do theological reflection.

One of the professors at ETS admitted that he couldn't deny what I said. "What degree," he asked, "do you offer at Southeastern for youth pastors?" I told him that we offered the perfect degree: the Master of Divinity!

There's a place for specialization, whether in education, music, youth, women's studies, and others, but not at the expense of significant biblical teaching. Think about it: a youth pastor teaches believers at a time when they are the most teachable and malleable. Those teaching youth should be the *most* skilled at teaching the Word, the best trained in theology, in the biblical languages, and in philosophy.

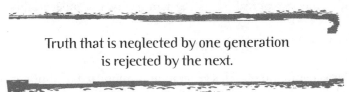

Truth that is neglected by one generation
is rejected by the next.

A postmodern culture awash in a sea of relativism needs truth to be proclaimed more, not less, clearly. Barna found that about half of America's teens believe that Jesus committed sins, and only about a third believes in hell. Truth that is neglected by one generation is rejected by the next. He adds, "While youth ministry has become a standard ministry program in tens of thousands of churches . . . there has been surprising little growth in the involvement of teenagers in the life of the Church over the past decade."[3]

I'm far from being the best youth speaker, but I've learned something in speaking to thousands of teens—they're hungry for the Word if we show them how it affects their lives. Barna's research echoes my conviction that after you get their attention, students still seek truth:

> When pressed to identify the single most important reason why [unchurched youth] attend a [church] youth group. . . . It turns

out that relationships bring the kids to the place, but they will
not return unless the church delivers the goods. What are they
looking for? Substance. Learning practical and credible insights
about God was listed twice as often as anything else as the most
important reason for returning. The fellowship, the games, the
music, the casual and friendly atmosphere—all those elements
are important to getting kids in the door—the first time. Getting them there on subsequent occasions requires those benefits
plus solid, personally applicable content.[4]

In other words, if you're going to feed youth spiritual Twinkies and
junk food when they need—and often long for—the meat of truth, leave
youth ministry and work in the nursery. Consider, the fastest-growing
soft drink in the youth population is Sprite. The company's ad cam-
paign says, "Image is nothing, thirst is everything—obey your thirst."
That's a message of realism. Give them reality, not superficiality.

We Must Teach, But How?

Barna has found that this generation is comprised of nonlinear thinkers who cut and paste their beliefs and values from a variety of sources.
They don't want to argue about moral absolutes. This means that they're
a generation comfortable with contradictions.

Richard Land, president of the Southern Baptist Convention's Ethics
and Religious Liberty Commission and host of "For Faith and Family,"
said this research regarding the Millennials shows America is cultivating
a generation of mainly right-brained thinkers.

"I just want to make sure," Land said, "that everybody understands
that this is a radical departure from Western thought, at least since the
time of the Renaissance." This way of thinking, he added, is so different
from that of other generations that it's like comparing a modern man to
one from medieval times.

Barna observed, "This calls into question, 'How do we teach young
people today?' Is preaching the best way to communicate God's truths
to them, at least the way we traditionally preach? How do we get them
to understand and embrace God's Word without ever compromising it

while still understanding [that youth] communicate very differently from previous generations?"[5] We can use the arts to present truth to a more right-brained generation, and we can also help students experience what they learn, so they make immediate application in a real world. But more than ever we need to teach the truth of Scripture to a youth culture bombarded with postmodern relativism. Strong, applicable, biblical preaching still communicates.

I recently wrote a book entitled *Radically Unchurched: Who They Are and How to Reach Them,*[6] which discusses how to communicate the gospel to an unchurched world. Inside our churches, however, we have another problem: too many people are radically *churched.* We've come to the place where Christianity is defined by behavior—going to church, giving money, serving in some way—instead of by belief. The long-term result is a form of Christianity tied to a building (the local church facilities, or the "edifice complex"), and one day a week (Sunday). But the Christianity of the New Testament sees the church as the people of God, 24/7, not a place or a time of the week. The Christianity of the New Testament flowed through believers, demonstrating a changed life, not churched behavior.

If we are to teach students the truths of the faith, we must do more than give them an anemic view of the body of Christ. We must teach in a way that helps them see the reality of Jesus every moment of every day, which includes both the imparting of truth (doctrine) and an ever-changing life (practice). Paul certainly emphasized both, and so should we.

Preaching Still Speaks

In practice, too many youth leaders portray a subtle skepticism about the power of the Word of God to change lives. A friend of mine is one of the most sought-after youth speakers in America. He makes presentations to over a hundred thousand teenagers and college students annually. Few on earth have ability comparable to his as an effective youth communicator. He's also somewhat unusual among speakers today. Why? Because he preaches straight, biblical, expository messages. And teenagers love it.

My friend is *both* a great youth speaker *and* an expositor, but an unwritten rule today apparently states that effective youth communicators must depend upon humor in lieu of the Bible. Many seem to believe that communicating to students and biblical exposition are mutually exclusive. Some even believe that preaching must be replaced by, or propped up with, drama. Now I love drama, and I'm a member of a church with one of the best drama ministries in America. Yet Christian *chic* need not replace Christian truth. What students need is not the latest quote from some teen magazine or a Tony-caliber play; they need the unsearchable riches of God.

One of the ways the youth group at our church dispenses these riches is through a quarterly panel discussion. We consistently open the Word and teach and preach. But four times a year we answer any and every question that youth have. This offers a different approach to communicating biblical truth and applying it where people live. (Hint: you can't do this without some people who know God's Word.)

It's time, then, to stop giving our children a heritage of biblical illiteracy. We should teach youth that biblical truth has nothing to fear. We should take on their hardest questions because, to rephrase a line from a movie, *They can handle the truth.* We should also provide youth with not only the best materials,[7] we should put the church's very best Bible teachers in the youth classes.

And if teaching the Bible means preaching the Bible, so be it. Youth do not hate preaching—they hate *boring* preaching. So do I. They can't stand services devoid of life and passion—neither can I. They need to see how truth connects to the real world, and be *challenged* to live that truth. We don't need to preach less; we need to apply more.

> Look closely at youth indicators, and you'll see
> that Millennial attitudes and behaviors represent a
> sharp break from Generation X, and are running exactly
> counter to trends launched by the Boomers. Across the
> board, Millennial kids are challenging a long list of
> common assumptions about what "postmodern" young
> people are supposed to become.[8]

Barna observes,

> Of the 22 million teens in the nation, nearly 15 million of them
> have some exposure to Christianity through youth groups . . .
> Why doesn't music alone attract them? Because they can usu-
> ally see better music elsewhere and in a more conducive envi-
> ronment. Why don't games serve as a sufficient allure? Because
> they can play games in many places—and usually have greater
> control over the nature and conduct of those experiences. Why
> won't they come if a lot of kids their own age are present? Be-
> cause it's the presence of their "tribe," not the mere presence of
> people from their generation, that makes the experience worth-
> while to them.[9]

The questions that Barna raises are serious, and he makes a significant point:

> I am convinced that we sometimes blur the distinction between
> what we have to do to attract teens to the church (i.e., marketing)
> and what we must do to impact them for Christ (i.e., ministry).
> Too often, it seems, we surrender ministry value for marketing
> impact—that is, we give up the responsibility to facilitate life
> change in order to succeed at attracting a crowd.
>   How do we do this? By performing music, dramas and offer-
> ing amusing teaching rather than engaging them in authentic
> worship and serious discipleship. By striving to facilitate rela-
> tionships rather than providing them with accountability. . . .
>   We have mastered the art of drawing a crowd, but at the
> expense of drilling deep into the lives of teenagers with spiritual
> truths. Games, loud music, interactive discussions, silly skits—
> all of those means have a place in youth ministry, but they must
> have a meaningful connection to the ultimate purpose of the
> ministry. If those approaches are justified solely because they
> help us to recruit a larger number of young people, then we will
> win the battle but lose the war.[10]

I took a vow during the summer of 1996 never to serve again as pastor at a youth camp. This wasn't because I hate teenagers or camps—on the contrary, I love them. My problem with youth camps is how they often fail to pour buckets of truth into students over a short period of time. I've heard all kinds of horror stories—camps that had leaders who lip sync contemporary pop artists, camps that replaced preaching with drama, camps that had all kinds of activities but very little content.

Then I went to a Go Tell Camp. Evangelist Rick Gage invited me to speak to the adult workers. The first night of the first camp Dr. James Merritt—president of the Southern Baptist Convention, and forty-something megachurch denominational pastor—preached. He preached the Word. He didn't play. He didn't tell jokes. He told it straight for forty-five minutes. And eighty-one students met the Lord that night.[11]

Quest Camps are another example of a ministry that raises the bar on strong preaching, authentic worship, and serious discipleship. A part of InQuest Ministries (www.inquest.org), these camps also feature the application of God's Word through creative means such as high ropes courses which teach teamwork and trust.

What About Sunday School?

Over the past several years, Sunday school in most churches has become the dead zone. Even after a whole weekend of youth meetings in which God moves and students get excited, they can walk into Sunday school and become zombies. What's happened to the excitement in the church about studying God's Word?

Recall that in past great awakenings a hunger for the Word was evident. John Wesley, for example, came to Christ at a small-group meeting in which the prologue to Luther's commentary on Romans was being read—not exactly the hottest youth communication package. Yet he met Christ, and God used him to rock England for Jesus. In the First Great Awakening in the American colonies, some people began to read the Scripture, commentaries, and sermons to one another. The hunger for the Word of God grew until "reading houses" were built to accommodate the numbers of people hungering for God's Word. That desire is evident, too, in Scripture. In Ezra's day the people stood half a day as the

Word was read and explained. Shouldn't our Sunday school teaching, then, undergo a reformation as well?—in our attitude and practice concerning Bible study.

Tips for Teachers

The following provides some practical insights for those who work with youth in Sunday school.

1. Teach the Bible, not your opinion of it. Do not sit in a circle and ask, "What does this passage say to you?" Ask what *God* is saying, and then apply it to the students' lives. Teaching the Bible is not the pooling of ignorance but the imparting of truth. Spurgeon is known for saying that the Bible is like a lion—you don't have to defend it, just turn it loose.

2. Remember, knowledge without application leads to frustration. When I was a "young preacher-boy" in college, I tried to meet every well-known preacher or professor I could, simply to ask for advice. When they had only a few moments to spare for me, I'd ask this question: "What one thing would you say to help a young preacher like me?"

I once met Dr. Barrymore White, an eminent Cambridge professor of church history and the principal of Regent's Park College. He visited our school to deliver a lecture, and after his lecture I asked Dr. White what advice he would give to me. I expected some lofty, brilliant exhortation that would be intellectually over my head. Instead, seemingly pleased by my query, the eminent scholar said, "Young man, the next time you are to preach, after you've prepared the message, studied the text, and are ready to deliver your address, stop for a few moments."

Smiling, he added, "Think about your subject, and then imagine—there's an elderly lady, recently widowed. She's come to hear from God. She hears your message and thinks, 'So what?' What will you say to her? There's also a youth, who comes to church alone. What will you say to him? Or to that young couple with their first child—what will you say to them? In other words, does your message, as biblical and as well developed as it may be, speak to the audience in a way that they can apply it to their lives?"

I've since developed what I call a "so what" approach to anything I teach. Do not misunderstand: the Word of God is truth, and always relates to real life. But if people don't make that connection, they miss the very truth they need so badly.

> Unless teenagers are provided with a very different spin on truth—one that is comprehensible, relevant, compelling, practical and consistently modeled—they can be expected to follow the path of least resistance—which is the path of relativism.[12]

This connection is what my friend Jeff Pratt refers to as "experience-based learning." Teachers must avoid the usual watered-down, emotional approach to teaching, and instead help students take the truth that is placed in their heads, move it to their hearts, and help them see how it changes their lives in the real world.

3. Atmosphere matters. Stanley and Hall note the importance of both the *context* and the *content* of youth ministry. They also note that most youth ministers work harder upon the former than upon the latter, spending much time on designing T-shirts and planning activities, and less time "determining what our students need to know before finishing high school."[13] While the emphasis on context over content is especially true when it comes to Wednesday nights, I wonder if both are given enough attention for Sunday morning Bible study.

Imagine these scenes:

- *Scene One:* You enter the classroom on Sunday morning. You're not prepared, you stayed up too late the night before, you didn't really like the lesson anyway, and your class attendance is down. You start by telling the class you're tired, ill prepared, and disappointed in them because they haven't brought any friends. The only enthusiasm you have is for the NFL game later, and you tell them.

- *Scene Two:* On Sunday morning you rise early to spend a little extra time in prayer for each student in your class. "I wonder if John will come today?" you ask yourself, praying that today John would come and meet Jesus. Having gone over the lesson, you ask God to let its truth penetrate your life. God gives you a glimpse of insight that excites you. You enter the classroom prayed up, fired up, and ready to challenge your students to be a little more like Jesus.

Do you think the two scenes above will affect the class differently? Of course they will! Each week, early in the week, ask God to make the lesson come alive for you. Seek a way for the lesson to help you better serve the Lord. Such earnest endeavor will spill over to your class. Other practical features add to atmosphere as well:

- Make the room as comfortable as possible.
- Get started on time.
- Be enthusiastic—it's contagious!
- Avoid embarrassing students—do not call on students to read the Bible or to pray publicly if they are easily embarrassed. Avoid other ways that unnecessarily single out people.
- Don't ask questions that have only a single correct answer. Try asking questions for which there are no wrong answers. For example, instead of asking, "Who was known as the encourager, and even had his name changed to that in the Bible?" Ask instead, "Can you name someone who has encouraged you? Tell me why or how?" *Then* introduce Barnabas as a biblical example. Such an approach encourages, rather than discourages, discussion.

That which we learn with delight we never forget.
—Aristotle

4. The secret to great teaching is contagion. "What you do screams so loud I cannot hear what you say," as Emerson is said to have stated. "Your people can tell when you have been much with God. That will be most in their ears that is most in your heart," stated Puritan pastor Richard Baxter. Young people will follow your example more than your teaching. If you are excited about the things of God, they'll eventually catch your passion.

5. See where your students could be, not where they are now. A great teacher sees the potential in students that they don't see in themselves. A missionary was once asked how he got so many young people—who, on the surface, had little potential—to do great things for God. His reply was, "I put a big crown over their head and help them grow into it." That's a teacher's calling.

6. Illustrate to educate. A great way to teach is by analogy. The Bible is full of stories, and youth love them.

7. Love your students. I probably have less in common with young people than most who read this book. I'm a middle-aged seminary professor. I live in the world of the academy. When I speak to students, I don't have automatic rapport with them. Many youth ministers seek out the "hot" speaker of the moment, adding to the insecurity of so many who teach the Bible to adults, confirming their fears that they can't communicate to youth. Paul was not the hottest thing going when he came to town. But he had the hand of God and a passion for those to whom he spoke.

If you teach to adults and don't have immediate rapport with students, it's not a big deal. Be real with them. Love them. Expect them to develop a love for God's Word.

MYTH OF YOUTH MINISTRY
The closer in age to youth the speaker is, the better he can communicate with them. No—communicating truth is not affected by age, but can be helped by maturity.

8. Start well and end well. Start your class with excitement. You have one hour a week to pour the Word of God into a group of young people—and it's an awesome honor. Because I don't have immediate rapport with students, I work very hard to get their attention in the first five minutes.

I may use a question, or an illustration, or an object lesson. I like to use self-deprecating humor. Remember, be yourself. InQuest Ministries, which provides the best Sunday school materials I've seen, offers excellent examples of ways to teach the Word effectively.

An old rule of thumb for teaching still applies: when you teach, tell them what you're going to tell them (give the point in a nutshell). Then tell them (teach the lesson). Then, tell them what you told them (summarize and apply). Creative repetition is a powerful way to teach.

End well. I try to finish every message or lesson with a real, specific point of application. Do not just teach on witnessing; give every student a gospel tract and challenge him or her to share it with someone. Don't just teach on forgiveness; ask students to write the name of someone they find it hard to forgive, and suggest ways to pray about forgiveness over the next week.

Here's one example. Let's say you're teaching a lesson at Christmastime. Challenge the students to turn one conversation during the next week from the secular—Santa, gifts, shopping—to the sacred—how God gave us Jesus. Remember, you, too, must do what you challenge them to do.

Twinkies or Truth?

While I'm on my travels my kids, Josh and Hannah, often ask me to bring back a surprise. Invariably my ten-year-old, Hannah, asks for candy. She loves candy (what kid doesn't), and like her dad, she's addicted to chocolate.

More times than not I get her and Josh a candy bar. I do believe in good nutrition, but I don't think an occasional candy bar will do much harm. But as much as Hannah loves candy, I think she'd love to live on a diet of M&Ms for breakfast, candy bars for lunch, and chocolate ice cream for supper. Such a diet would soon wreak havoc with her blood sugar level, as well as robbing her of essential nutrients.

I'm afraid, though, that much of youth ministry in our churches has fed teenagers a spiritual diet of Twinkies and bonbons while avoiding the prime rib of truth. I'm convinced that this biblical malnourishment is not intentional but comes from good motives mixed with bad judgment—like parents who want to do a good job of raising their kids but have no awareness of what that entails.

In my travels and interaction with student ministers and youth, I'm struck by how often the emphasis is on effective communication with teens while *what* is being communicated is virtually ignored. The result is a focus on how to get the message across, which de-emphasizes the message itself. McLuhan was wrong—the medium is *not* the message.

I don't want to sound like a naysayer or a critic from the ivory towers. I don't know any youth pastors who have a goal of raising up a generation of spiritually anemic students. But what if youth pastors decided to set a new standard, where the youth ministry was built on biblical teaching and everything else revolved around it? Games could still be played, fellowship encouraged, drama teams sent forth—while biblical Christians are being grown. What if youth pastors and other leaders—including parachurch and denominational leaders—were handed a spiritual food chart that illustrated the essential food groups required to grow radical, dynamic believers? Would our students be considered healthy?

Resource

InQuest

Every time you meet with youth you should teach some biblical truth. No, you don't have to preach before the volleyball game. But in some way, every time you meet, find a way to communicate truth. That being said, the best place to teach biblical truth week after week is still the Sunday school, and curriculum tends to be the biggest struggle for pastors and youth pastors.

As stated above, the best literature I've seen is produced by InQuest Ministries. My church uses it, and increasingly churches across America are utilizing these excellent resources. Without compromising the value of teaching biblical truth, InQuest resources stress learning *and* living biblical truth.

InQuest bases its approach on three "cries" of today's student, which are adapted from Josh McDowell's book *The Disconnected Generation*.[14]

1. *Love and care.* "If I were asked to identify the core reason that young people are succumbing to the lure of a godless culture and lashing out with rage, I would say that it is that they feel alone and disconnected."

2. *Truth to base his or her life upon.* "I have concluded that unless our students become convinced of the truth and credibility of their faith, when something more exciting or emotionally stimulating comes along, they will change their belief and abandon whatever Christian faith they do have."

3. *A model to follow.* "Students are no longer asking which faith is true or most credible, but which faith works for them. So to take our students beyond subjective believism, we must not only show that Christianity works, but we must also show that it actively works because it is true."[15]

In response to the three "cries," InQuest follows a threefold teaching model to reach today's postmodern, Millennial youth:

Convergence
Definition: To find a common point
Goal: To connect with and touch the heart
Biblical Model: Jesus touched them (Mark 1:40–42)
Need Met: Provide love and care

Students are looking for someone to touch their hearts before that person attempts to open their minds. Each lesson begins with connecting points that allow the teacher to start creating an experience for the student. As we touch the heart we open the mind.

Transference
Definition: To give away something of value
Goal: To impart to and open the mind
Biblical Model: Jesus taught them (Mark 9:31)
Need Met: Truth to base their lives upon

Students today live in the karaoke culture. They would rather be participators than spectators.

Confluence
Definition: A coming together at one point
Goal: To impact and change lives
Biblical Model: Jesus challenged them (John 8:11)
Need Met: A model to follow[16]

Confluence refers to a point where two rivers join to become one. How excited young Timothy must have been to see his model Paul share how the truth was working in his life. Students will be given the opportunity each week to apply imparted truth to their daily lives.

What's the best way, then, to impart biblical knowledge to Millennials? If we teach with love, if we teach biblical truth and model that truth, we will teach our children well.

Chapter Nine

Get Real
Authentic Living

But you shall receive power when the Holy Spirit has come
upon you; and you shall be witnesses to Me in Jerusalem,
and in all Judea and Samaria, and to the end of the earth.
—Acts 1:8

I love reptiles—from the little ring-necked snakes in our backyard to the big gators at the zoo. Ever since I was a preteen I've been fascinated with snakes, lizards, alligators, and turtles. At one time or another I've kept most types of snakes that were native to where I lived—rat snakes, garter snakes, king snakes, water snakes, even a copperhead! I've held a black mamba in Africa, caught water moccasins, and taken hold of snapping turtles as big as a garbage can lid. More recently, I've kept everything from ball, Burmese, rock, and carpet pythons to corn snakes and an anaconda. Over one summer I once had a monitor lizard named Goliath. He was so big we had to walk him on a leash like a dog.

With that background, you can imagine my favorite program. That's right—the Crocodile Hunter. I just love to watch Steve Irwin do everything except get eaten by a massive saltwater crocodile. The show has risen from obscurity on the Animal Planet cable network to the point where Irwin has been featured in his own movie. I've met people from all over the globe, as far away as China, who know of the Croc Hunter.

It may sound like a stretch, but in a way, the spreading fame of the Crocodile Hunter parallels the growing passion of youth to do something that matters. How?

First, Steve Irwin is a *radical*. None of this film-from-a-safe-distance, telephoto lens business. More than one camera has been cracked by a croc bite. Irwin's no professional photographer, but he's a radical when it comes to his love for reptiles. Young people long to live for something with such radical abandon.

Second, Steve Irwin is *real.* Watch his show long enough and you learn about him from his earliest croc capture, to his wedding, to the birth of his first child. He lets you in on the everyday world in which he lives. His show is not a Hollywood set; it's the real world of Australia. No doubt some of his captures were set up, and the adventures at times may be overplayed, but what you see is pretty much for real. And young people crave that—the up close and personal.

Very little matches the up close of a snake hunt, and I've been on real snake hunts. Using a snake stick, I recently caught a big water moccasin. He was striking everywhere—biting himself and the stick; venom was everywhere—talk about an adrenaline rush! But this is not the greatest rush I ever experienced. No, nothing in this life compares to the joy of winning someone to Jesus. We need to let young people in on this rush. The best way to teach youth to witness is to get them out there doing it. That makes Christianity less an institution and more a lifestyle.

Third, Steve Irwin is a *risk taker.* What a thrill I had catching that angry cottonmouth moccasin. That snake was trying to kill me! But unlike Irwin, I caught the snake from a safe distance, a yard away, with a snake stick. None of the "break off a bushy branch" and catch him with your bare hands for me! If we challenged students to take risks, to get out of the boat like the apostle Peter did, and to take risks for God, we'd be amazed at what they could do!

The Contagious Power of Evangelism

A few years ago I spoke to a church with a fabulous youth group. The teens there seemed to have an unusual love for God. Their youth pastor set a high bar for them, had them in the Word, and their spiritual depth impressed me. On the last night, I challenged the church to take gospel tracts and share them with someone the next week. The response was terrific. Some of the youth had asked for my e-mail address, and one student e-mailed me, asking how to witness to a friend named John. I sent a long e-mail, explaining ways to share Christ with him. She forwarded it to John. While that wasn't my plan, it worked—for John met Jesus after that. In the days that followed, the students shared, as did their pastor, exciting stories. The bottom line is, in less than a week, a total of five people accepted Christ, simply because young people shared.

Two weeks later I was in Atlanta, Georgia, and picked up a copy of *USA Today.* The headline told of a different group of students in Arkansas. Westside Middle School in Jonesboro appeared to be a typical public school in a small city in northeastern Arkansas. But what happened on Tuesday, March 24, 1998, was anything but typical. *USA Today's* headline told the story: "Five Killed at Ark. School: 4 Students, Teacher Die In Ambush; 2 Classmates Held."

The premeditated ambush on classmates by two boys, eleven and thirteen years old, sent shockwaves across the nation. The very day this happened, my son, Josh, had accompanied me to Atlanta. The two of us visited Zoo Atlanta, ate hot dogs at the Varsity, and shopped at the Underground. At the same time in Arkansas, those boys pulled the school fire alarm at Westside, hid behind trees with rifles and, in camouflage gear, shot at people as they filed out of the building. They killed five and wounded fourteen others.

All this because one of the boys was upset with his former girlfriend. And yet two weeks earlier, the small youth group I'd met with led five to Jesus. The gospel matters!

In the church, we are quite adept at shaking our fist at the shadowy side of society. We hurl names at the cultural darkness of our day, throwing rocks into the pit of contemporary ungodliness. But the way to remove darkness is to turn on the Light. None of us as individuals can change society as a whole, but we can change *our* world. We can't touch the life of every troubled youth, but we can influence the life of some young person. We can challenge youth to be witnesses, to live authentic lives that count for something

This is not a day for building youth ministry on entertainment, yet that seems to be the rage. We must instead place greater emphasis on taking the zeal of youth and channeling it into adventurous and challenging opportunities like evangelism. We have an opportunity to affect a significant part of the youth culture through our churches. So instead of trying to out-world the world, why not challenge youth to experience the adventure of a radically changed life through Christ?

The International Mission Board of the Southern Baptist Convention commissions hundreds of new missionaries annually. As of spring 2003, the two commissioning services with the greatest number of missionaries appointed at one time were the services immediately after the terrorist attack on September 11, 2001, and immediately after Operation Iraqi Freedom in early 2003. During the Iraqi war more people signed up for military service as well. Why do more people surrender to international missions and to the military in times of danger? Because something inside all of us makes us want to *do* something. Youth want to make an impact, so let's feed their zeal to change the world.

To follow up with you, our adults and students had a great time. Several adults came to me and told me they really enjoyed your talks. We held a guys' Bible study throughout October—last night was the last one, and some of the students there wanted to keep it going, using the *Light the Fire* book they read. So our students' leaders will be leading that!

One of the girls called me last night because she had the *Light the Fire* book at school and was reading it, when her friend started asking her about it. She was able to lead that girl to the Lord there in school! She called to tell me because that was the first person she personally won to Christ. Our servant leaders, when they met with me that Saturday morning, wanted to know more about evangelism training, so we'll be beginning that as well.

Michael

This e-mail from a youth pastor in Florida represents the experience of many others who have discovered the passion that youth have for the gospel—once they see its power. Young people will rise to the level to which they are challenged, but if unchallenged, they'll discover their own challenges, many of which are destructive. Why not show them a better way? Help them see the adventurous challenge of taking up their cross and following Jesus.

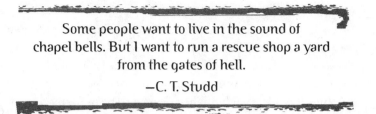

Some people want to live in the sound of
chapel bells. But I want to run a rescue shop a yard
from the gates of hell.
—C. T. Studd

One of the most practical ways to train youth in evangelism is through a strategy called the NET. The NET teaches and encourages the witness to share the gospel in the context of his or her testimony. The NET especially relates to the postmodern world in which we live by its emphasis on relationships and the story of the gospel. You can find out more about it at www.namb.net, at the link to evangelism resources.

Here's an e-mail from a Korean student who found the NET to be helpful.

From: Jane
To: Mitch

Hi!

Guess what happened yesterday? After school, three of my friends and I went to Pizza Hut. On the way to Pizza Hut, we talked about what we're planning to do over the winter break. I said I was so excited because I was going to the winter retreat with my church. Then they asked what I was going to do, where I was going, etc. Monica asked what religion I was in, specifically. So I said I'm a Christian. She looked like she was thinking deeply about that. So I asked what she thinks will happen after she dies. I said, "I used to be not sure about what was going to happen to me. In fact, I didn't even know the reason for living." I went on with my testimony. I was so thrilled. After the practices that we did in the NET, it really did become easier to tell, and the testimony was smoother, and it included the verses and the facts about Jesus. I talked for a long time. I really shared a lot about what I thought. They seemed kind of shocked, but at the same time relieved and more comfortable talking with me b/c I opened myself up. Then they started telling me about their life and problems. They were so personal and shocking to me. They were so real and so different from what I thought of them in class. We finished our conversation with my suggestions of thinking about eternal life. They seemed to be in deep thought, and I was thankful and amazed. I told them so much about myself and we really got close to each other. We promised to go out together more often. Yesterday was one of the most important days of my life. I really thank God, and I'm really excited to see my friends. I hope and pray that I won't disappoint them with my behavior. Please pray for me that I can somehow make a difference in my friends' lives and help them to meet God. Thank you and talk to you later!

This young witness demonstrates the passion of youth—once they are trained and encouraged—for sharing Christ. Barna, in an extensive survey of this generation, observed, "Mosaics [i.e., Millennials] will provide the Church with a massive and fertile population for evangelism and discipleship."[1] But it may also produce the most zealous witnesses of any generation. And their zeal is much needed. The Millennials are the most unevangelized population of students in recent history.

> Brethren, do something, do something, do something. While committees waste their time over resolutions, do something. While societies and unions are making constitutions, let us win souls. Too often we discuss, and discuss, and discuss, and Satan laughs in his sleeve. I pray you be men of action all of you.[2]

Intentional Evangelism

Imagine a new football coach at the local high school who begins two daily practices with great zeal, working the students to exhaustion. After weeks of such practice, he tells the team, "I've decided that we won't have any games this year. Instead, we're only going to practice the entire season."

Having played football, I can tell you such a statement would demoralize the team. You practice so you can *play*. But this is precisely how the church often treats youth. We teach them to share their faith, but do we let them in the game? Do we take them out into the world to put their training to the test?

My son, Josh, is now a youth. During one period of time, he led more people to Christ than I did. Several in our youth group have, in fact, led people to Christ. How? Every Sunday night our youth go witnessing. We have a big crowd every week, and Josh hates to miss it. Personal witnessing is one bar we've raised for our students.

I've learned something over the past three years. I'd never spend an entire weekend with students without involving them in evangelism. *Never.* As I began to speak more and more at youth events, I made a commitment that if we had a youth weekend, such as a DiscipleNow, we'd give strong emphasis to prayer, to worship, to biblical preaching and teaching—and to evangelism. We always have students go out witnessing on Saturdays. Many of these youth who go for their first time ever don't want to stop when the time is up for witnessing! I've received dozens of e-mails from young people on fire for the Lord and who are leading their peers to Christ because they learned to witness by witnessing.

Kelly Green has capitalized on this emerging generation's desire to change their world. Green has organized Frontliners, a summer ministry that involves about four thousand youth in various venues who spend an entire week of their summer street witnessing.[3] Rick Gage's Go Tell Camps also include a time of witnessing in the local community on Thursday afternoon.

Christian clubs are organizing at public schools these days, and I applaud this development. In the 1970s I helped start a Christian club at my school that became the largest organization on campus. It's unfortunate, though, that most of the youth groups are merely clubs for Christians. Do any of these groups have a burden to reach the teeming masses of teenagers and lead them to Christ? From my experience in speaking to youth, Christian young people have the burden, but they have not been trained and encouraged to evangelize. I totally agree with the following quote by Len Taylor and Richard Ross:

> By mobilizing [students'] efforts and empowering them to be missionaries, they can be Great Commission Christians, accomplishing the work of ministry. Sometimes we sell short the capabilities of these youths and fail to equip them for ministry. The church needs youth ministry built on new principles. Drawing a crowd is not enough. We have been good at drawing crowds of youth. But, if pizza gets them to church, what will take them out?[4]

"A.K.A. Your Public School"

Years ago, Audio Adrenaline wrote a great song called "A.K.A. Your Public School." In it they sing, "They pay to put you in the classes / it's your chance to reach the masses." The public school classroom is the greatest mission field in America. A campus missionary strategy for students already exists (see www.signofthefish.com). Perhaps it's time to train and commission as missionaries Christian adults who teach in public schools.

Taylor and Ross, both veterans of years of ministry to students, make the point well:

> Do you know where 95 percent of all youth can be found 7 hours a day, 5 days a week, 9 months a year for seven years of their life? And no, it's not their bed. It's their school campus. . . . We must go where they are.
>
> Let's face it, youth are not breaking down the doors of our churches to get there. As the teenage population continues to rise, we continue to fall further and further behind in reaching youth. Could it be that we are trying to reach them where the majority cannot be found?[5]

You Are Not Neutral

As a youth leader you will never be neutral. You are either leading people to know Jesus better, or you are nudging them away from Him. And because the passion that youth bring to witnessing can affect a whole church, the stakes are simply too high for us to be indifferent toward teaching them evangelism.

Greg Stier writes, "A handful of students in one dead church can remind the adults of what this Christianity thing is all about." I've personally seen this happen on a number of occasions. "Passionate evangelism," writes Stier, "burning in the hearts of on-fire teens can set a whole congregation ablaze."[6]

Sounds exciting, doesn't it? And youth love excitement. Barna notes that youth "crave unique and fun experiences,"[7] and this craving is a great advantage for the church, if we'd just wake up. We don't have to teach teenagers how to have fun, but we can coach them, show them how to *redefine fun.* On the numerous occasions when I've taken teenagers out to share their faith, their hearts race and their knees knock. They're terrified. But over and over again after these students have gone out to share their faith, they've come back with an adrenaline rush, in such excitement, giving each other high fives, hugging each other, not wanting to stop, excited about the next time they'll get an opportunity to do that.

In Wisconsin, I heard about a group of teenagers who were taught one year about sharing their faith. When the classes were over they asked, "Now that we've learned this, why don't we go out and practice it?" The youth encouraged the adults who led them, and they went out to share the gospel. They had an incredible time.

No, we don't need to teach young people how to have fun; we need to teach them how living for Jesus is the greatest ride you can ever take. We need to show them that whenever you step out of your comfort zone into new, exciting, and even frightening situations—situations in which you have to depend upon the Lord—the level of fun is not of this world.

If you haven't noticed, young people *love* to talk about spiritual things. Saved youth do. Lost youth do. You don't have to be a slick salesman to get into a gospel conversation. You don't have to be clever. Just be real.

If you're a youth leader who hasn't led your students in witnessing because *you* are afraid or feel unprepared, here's some advice:

1. *Be honest.* Tell your students you're learning. They want a real person, not superman.
2. *Be a learner.* Learn to share your faith. For starters, check out Greg Stier's book *Outbreak*.
3. *Be a grower.* Let them see you're willing to grow and be changed.

While you're learning and growing, share the gospel in your youth meetings. Teach the Word, but include the gospel in your teaching. Why? Over 80 percent of professions of faith occur before age twenty. And Barna found that about half of the youth who call themselves Christians and participate in youth groups in a typical month are not actually believers. That means around seven million unsaved youth are in church regularly.[8]

Charles Haddon Spurgeon, the prince of preachers, said to exegete the text, expound the Scriptures, and plow a furrow to the cross. How sad would it be for a student to bring a lost friend to the youth meeting, and then the speaker doesn't offer the gospel.

Church members, adults and youth, must be prepared to welcome lost youth. Lost youth are going to act lost because they are! One Sunday I was approached by a deacon of the church where I was serving. He came to tell me a few youth were skateboarding in front of our worship center. A nearby elderly lady said, "We need to put up a sign indicating there is to be no skate boarding." Fortunately I had a pastor who looked for a teachable moment. He began that morning worship service off with these words: "There are some young people here that we have been trying to get to come to our church for weeks. Isn't that great that they are here today?" He invited them to bring their friends the next week. He also said he would meet them after church for an exhibition of their skateboarding talents![9]

Get Real About Love

Teach your youth not only to invite their lost friends but to be patient with them. A tremendous need is evident in youth groups, for example to teach young ladies biblical modesty in their dress. But a lost young lady need not be singled out for her attire if she doesn't know any better. Note: Christian young ladies should! Teach guys to behave like gentlemen, but exercise gentleness if an unruly student shows up who has no idea how to act in church.

Douglas Hyde notes how Communists appealed to the idealism of youth: "The Communists' appeal to idealism is direct and audacious. They say that if you make mean little demands upon people, you will get a mean little response which is all you deserve, but if you make big demands on them, you will get a heroic response."[10]

Get Real About Rejection

I recently began utilizing an idea I got from Greg Stier's *Dare 2 Share Training*. When youth return from witnessing encounters, inevitably some have been slammed (*slammed* means to have a door slammed in your face). So Stier applauds those teams as graduates of "Persecution University." Jesus said, did he not, that we are blessed when we are persecuted (Matt. 5). So I keep a tally at report time of not only how many times the gospel was shared, but of how many had doors slammed in their faces, or got chased by a dog, or got cursed for the sake of the gospel.

Persecution is a good thing. It binds people together like nothing else. Let a band of teens get radical for the gospel and face ridicule. They will bind together. Want to find a group of believers who really understand fellowship? Find a group facing persecution—they *need* each other.

Get Real About the Gospel

Stier's *Dare 2 Share* approach is another excellent way to involve youth in witnessing. His approach includes *Prayer* (praying for lost friends), *Dare* (challenging lost friends to come to church to hear the gospel), and

Share (unleashing youth to witness to their peers). The approach *Dare 2 Share* uses in witnessing follows the acrostic GOSPEL:

- God created us to be with Him;
- Our sins separate us from God;
- Sins cannot be removed by good deeds;
- Paying the price for sin, Jesus died and rose again;
- Everyone who trusts in Him alone has eternal life;
- Life that is eternal can never be lost.[11]

Stier, who has spent much more time than I have with youth pastors, asks of youth pastors a series of sobering questions, paraphrased below:

1. When is the last time you shared your faith?
2. Do you talk about evangelism more than you do it?
3. Are you so busy doing good things you can't do great things (like witnessing)?
4. Are you so busy studying the latest youth fad or technology that you fail to study the Scriptures to get a word from God?
5. Do you burn with a passion to reach every lost youth in your area for Christ?[12]

During one youth weekend, the group divided into teams, and we went door-to-door to share Christ. I took the two most frightened students—two ninth-grade girls—on my team because I like to do the talking. We had an uneventful afternoon, until we came to a home where a big, elderly gentleman answered the door. When I introduced us and named the church, he retorted angrily, "I don't like that church!" I've done a lot of door-to-door witnessing, and I had a hunch he was just having a good time with us.

The two young ladies, though, had faces as white as sheets. They hadn't caught on to the guy and thought he was Satan incarnate!

"I bet you're a member of that church, aren't you?" I asked.

He chuckled, and said, "Yes, I am." We all had a good laugh once the girls figured out he was only kidding.

Several months later one of those young ladies e-mailed me, thanking me for teaching her how to witness. And then she added, "Because of what I learned, I've led two of my friends to Christ."

That's what can happen when we show youth what it means to get real, when we model authentic witnessing. Evangelism is caught more than it is taught.

Chapter Ten

Every Move I Make

Authentic Worship

I beseech you therefore, brethren, by the mercies of God, that you present your bodies a living sacrifice, holy, acceptable to God, which is your reasonable service. And do not be conformed to this world, but be transformed by the renewing of your mind, that you may prove what is that good and acceptable and perfect will of God.
—Romans 12:1–2

Cassie Bernall would have graduated from Columbine High School with the class of 2000—had she lived to see that day. But on that tragic day in 1999, Cassie said yes when her classmate asked if she believed in God. Now she wears a martyr's crown. Why did she say yes? Because during a time of worship at a youth retreat her life was radically changed. Her friend Jamie recalls that night:

> There was a nighttime praise-and-worship service. I don't remember what the guy talked about, though the theme of the weekend was overcoming the temptations of evil and breaking out of the selfish life. It was the singing that for some reason just broke down Cassie's walls. It really seemed to change her. I wasn't expecting much out of the whole thing, also not for her, because she'd always been so closed. I thought, *Just one weekend is not going to change her, though it could help.* So when she totally broke down, I was pretty shocked.
> Actually we were outside the building, and Cassie was crying. She was pouring out her heart—I think she was praying—

and asking God for forgiveness. Inside a lot of kids had been bringing stuff up to the altar—drug paraphernalia and stuff like that; they were breaking off their old bonds.[1]

Jamie comments on the change in perspective brought about by that night. The two girls and a few others went to the top of a mountain and gazed at the greatness of God. "We just stood there in silence for several minutes, totally in awe of God. It was phenomenal—our smallness, and the bigness of the sky. The bigness of God was so real," Jamie recalled. "Later I noticed that Cassie's whole face had changed. . . . It was like her eyes were more hopeful. There was something new about her."[2]

Chapter 7 made the point that worship is less a corporate act that can be done privately, and more a private act that can be done corporately. So one's daily walk with God is critical to one's corporate worship. And corporate worship has a powerful role in the life of a believer. This role is even more powerful with youth, who thrive on meetings—such as worship services—for encouragement and edification. One of the most obvious shifts I've seen in today's churched youth is, in fact, their passion in corporate worship.

Worship involves far more, however, than a service or music. Worship is a lifestyle, not just a one-hour meeting in a particular building. In the book of Romans, Paul offers first in 12:1–2 a biblical paradigm for worship. Then in chapters 1–11 Paul's vast theological treatise shows how biblical orthodoxy (right belief) and orthopraxy (right practice) come together in worship. In its essence, then, worship has nothing to do with either a church building, a certain time or day of the week, or music. It has to do with offering ourselves to God.

The Dominant Role of Music

A new type of worship movement has spread through the church in the past decade. Central to this is the rise of new songs such as "I Could Sing of Your Love Forever" and "Shout to the Lord." These new songs include Scripture choruses such as "Better Is One Day," contemporary hymns such as "I Come by the Blood," and remakes of old hymns: "I'm Forgiven," for example, which is taken from Wesley's "And Can It Be";

and "Wonderful Cross" added to "When I Survey." The proliferation of screens for the words and the growing number of praise teams has resonated well with youth. In the 1970s the Jesus Movement turned the youth choir into a dominant force in many churches. Now, praise bands offer an avenue for students to participate in services.

"Perhaps the most underestimated influence on the lives of teens is their music," Barna has found, adding, "Our research confirms that music may be the single, most important cultural creation of a generation, a special form of communication that is theirs forever, even if it is borrowed or mimicked by others."[3] He further observes,

> For teenagers, music is much more than mere entertainment or a diversion from the stress of homework, household chores and worries about the future. For millions of young people, music produces a life philosophy for them to consider and follow; cultural heroes and role models to look up to and imitate; values and lifestyles to embrace; a common language to employ that sets them apart and provides a distinctive identity; and the opportunity to develop community related to a shared sense of common sound, ideas or artists.[4]

Yet parents by the thousands, if not millions, have no idea what their children listen to. Even Christian parents are lacking in discernment concerning the type of music their children hear. If music plays a dominant role in shaping the worldview, mind-set, and philosophy of teenagers, certainly parents should dialogue with their young people about the influence of music.

MTV well understands the impact of music. When MTV was formed its vision was to be more, in fact, than a music channel. Its vision was to create a distinct subculture promoted by music. I'm no fan of MTV, but you can't deny their success in creating a subculture. We can learn from MTV without buying into their often anti-Christian positions.

That being said, since music is a huge factor in the lives of youth and in corporate worship, shouldn't we be teaching how music has a role in worship? I love a lot of contemporary Christian music (CCM), and I play the bass guitar in chapel at my seminary. A band called Joy Made

Full often travels with me, and we have a blast leading people in worship musically.

But do youth ministers take the time to help students discern good from evil, not only in secular music, but in Christian music as well? Do we lower the bar to mediocrity by simply covering our youth rooms with posters of the latest Christian groups? Or do we help students learn the difference between groups with integrity and a heart for ministry, and groups in the "industry" with a knack for entertainment? More important, in the music we use, are we teaching young people to worship God? When the second most consistent source of theology comes from the songs we sing in church, do we assess the content in any consistent manner?

> Jesus did not intend His church merely to provide bigger and better amusement for bigger and more upscale audiences. His vision was of a church that would inject His light and life into a dark and dying world. So we had better take the vision of Jesus seriously, or we won't just be amusing ourselves to death. We'll be amusing people to hell.

Worship Services Connecting with Youth

Much has been written about the postmodern world in which we live. One of the marks of postmodern youth is a desire for authentic experiences. When visiting youth come to your regular youth service or Bible study, what do they find? When they join you for worship on Sunday, do they sense the presence of God? Is meeting God a priority of those times? In other words, do visiting youth leave with a sense of their having met with God?

Any time corporate worship happens—at your church on Sunday morning or at a youth service—a genuine encounter with God can make a huge mark on students. The singing should open the hearts of those present. The ministry of the Word should give unambiguous truth applied to life in a real world. Such a focus can have a profound effect on both saved and lost young people.

How, though, does a service open the door to that genuine encounter with God? Not by repeating the same choruses again and again, like a Buddhist chant. The prophets of Baal on Mt. Carmel, who incessantly chanted the same thing over and over, are *not* our model. Encountering God *can* happen through the joy of praises sung to God. But genuine encounter is more likely to happen if the singing springs from the sense of awe at a great God, who is evident in the lives of youth. Is there something real in your youth's corporate worship? Is there a sense of the manifest presence of God?

Over the past several years, I've observed a change in youth groups—in their desire to connect with God. I used to break the ice or build rapport with youth by playing games. Recently, however, I've found that simply leading youth in praise and worship music does the same thing, but it appeals to the best in youth, not the worst. And the music used in services can also connect with unchurched youth. Barna found that, of teens who purchased contemporary Christian music, one out of every three was not born again. Overall, about one of every ten non-Christian teens and one in three Christian teens bought a Christian recording. So roughly one million teenagers who claim not to be a born-again Christians bought at least one contemporary Christian recording. One might argue, then, that music is the most significant inroad of the Christian faith into the life of youth.[5]

I was just at a church in Texas where a young man was led to Christ from a totally unchurched background. The witnessing team that led him to Jesus found him listening to Christian music!

A Worship Revolution in Our Time

Do your students enjoy CCM or love to sing praise and worship choruses? Do you listen to a CCM station? Neither CCM nor CCM stations could be found before the late 1960s. As noted in chapter 6, the Jesus Movement of the '70s made a huge impact on worship in the local church, and especially in the area of music.

Churches struggled with this—an electric guitar in church was considered to some a sign of the Antichrist. And when drums entered our sanctuary, not everyone was pleased! Consider, though, that every time in history God has moved in great revival, music in the church changes. The psalmist understood this when he wrote about a new song in Psalm 33:3. In the 1700s, Charles Wesley wrote over six thousand hymns, changing the face of music in England. In the 1970s, Scripture, folk music, and pop music came together to form a whole new kind of music that was simpler and more contemporary. This new music became a natural part of Jesus Movement worship.

In the less formal setting of coffeehouses and communes, contemporary rock music was easily transformed into Jesus rock music. In Nashville, the Koinonia coffeehouse was seminal in the rise of CCM. Several groups got their start at The Adam's Apple coffeehouse in Fort Wayne, Indiana, and many are still playing. The best known is the Christian rock group Petra. Likewise, the Jesus festivals provided a forum for musicians to share their songs.

Many of the early CCM singers were rock artists who began singing Christian themes after their conversion. Four of the members of the pop group Love Song, for example, became Christians at Calvary Chapel, Costa Mesa, California. The group then began singing songs at Calvary Chapel that they'd written about faith in Christ.

To keep abreast of the new musical form, the magazine *Contemporary Christian Music* was founded in 1978. A sort of Christian *Billboard* magazine, it included record charts. Don Francisco's "He's Alive" was the first number one song, and the Second Chapter of Acts' "Mansion Builder" was the first top-selling album. The publication also has a radio countdown (20: The Countdown Magazine) and a televised video channel (CCM-TV). Since the Jesus Movement, the number of CCM radio stations has continued to grow, and Paul Baker was an early leader in the field, being the first to air an "all-Jesus rock radio show" in St. Petersburg, Florida.

The music gave a spiritual compass to a generation who at times felt left out of the institutional church. It helped to make the spiritual commitment of the youth more than a Sunday-only experience. As Styll put it, "It's made Christianity relevant for them. . . . Christian music is viable for the other six days of the week, not just Sunday morning."[6] So in one sense, CCM helped to do what many churches at the time had neglected—depict Christianity as a daily lifestyle, not a weekly meeting.

The music arising out of the Jesus Movement led to innovations which were also useful in reaching others.[7] One of the ways music changed worship was in the youth musicals. God was at work with teenagers in the '70s, and one way He worked was through music. Youth choir tours covered America and Canada, becoming the most effective evangelistic tool of youth groups during that time. For example, in Bridgeport, Connecticut, the 104-voice youth choir from First Baptist, Hendersonville, North Carolina, sang twice daily at a weeklong "Festival of Faith" crusade. Some 120 persons made professions of faith. Merchants in the shopping center where the choir sang wrote letters stating that the choir performances "brought a feeling of good cheer in an area where crime had given shoppers [a] sense of uneasiness."[8] Folk youth musicals exploded in number in the late 1960s. Southern Baptists were the major leaders in the early youth musicals, and youth choir tours were more prominent in the early 1970s than at any time before or since.

Not only Southern Baptists, but Charismatics, Methodists, and many others were in the middle of the dramatic changes taking place. Philip Landgrave commented in 1972 that "in just three years, a dramatic change has taken place in the youth music scene of many congregations."[9] He added that a variety of contemporary expressions, from folk to rock to country & western, had suddenly become acceptable in the worship of traditional and nontraditional churches. Forrest H. Heeren, former dean of the school of music at Southern Baptist Seminary, said in the 1970s that musical instruments such as guitars, "which ten to fifteen years ago would have been severely questioned are now brought into the regular church service."[10]

What began in coffeehouses on weeknights, then, has evolved into a fresh wind of worship blowing through congregations on Sundays. Contemporary Christian music and the influx of new styles of music into many churches has led in recent years to the creation of not only new praise and worship music but a whole new world of church music in general. Now, CCM stations fill the airwaves with praise and worship songs created for not only radio listening but for corporate worship. Even groups like Third Day, who rose to popularity as a Christian rock band, have seen their greatest influence come by releasing CDs filled with praise and worship music. Bands formed not to do concerts but lead people in congregational worship are some of the most popular today.

Worship Changes for Better or Worse

But recall, everything with the potential for good also has the potential for harm. Not all the music was good, and not all CCM today honors Christ. Nor does every new praise and worship song magnify Christ. The early musicians in the Jesus Movement would often drive across the country and sing for no pay. But today CCM has become an industry, and the "artists" (formerly known as ministers) too often more resemble pop icons in culture than the Lord they claim to serve. One band leader, in fact, said, "You can't talk about God too much when you sing. It doesn't pay the bills." Some today have forgotten the reason we sing. And it's a sad commentary on CCM that some of the better known musicians have brought dishonor to God by immoral behavior. Most musicians and singers, though, still sing praises to God with great joy.

While CCM began in part as a protest against dead church services that dishonored God by their lack of passion for Him, CCM has itself become, like other movements that began as a protest against institutionalism, institutionalized. Now a multimillion-dollar industry with its own awards program (the Gospel Music Association's Dove Awards, which now has thirty-three categories) and a category in the Grammies, the genre has established itself as a power in the music industry. From 1980 to 1990, while the overall music industry doubled its revenue, gospel music, in particular contemporary Christian, nearly tripled from $180 million to $500 million. The industry of today looks alarmingly like the establishment the early Christian artists so vehemently opposed. The power of fame and fortune can easily push praise and worship music to the margins of truth.

> Be careful of loving music that is called Christian because it sounds like the music of the world with an occasional reference to God. Contemporary music in itself is not necessarily good or bad; the lyrics make the difference.

One reason that CCM has become institutionalized is a shift in its development. In its early days, CCM was primarily evangelistic in nature, trying to reach seekers and nonbelievers. Then as new record labels were born, Christian radio stations emerged across the country, Christian book and record stores increased in numbers, and a concert network developed, the audience shifted to primarily Christians. As Styll put it, "Before long, contemporary Christian music had almost totally abandoned its original call to influence popular culture and had become a subculture in and of itself."[11]

Such was not what gave birth to the music coming out of the Jesus Movement. In the 1970s, most musicians and singers simply sought to honor Christ in their music, and to do so in a way that communicated with their peers. Those who continue with that passion are experiencing God in new and incredible ways. Many CCM record labels still place a premium on the spiritual commitment of its artists. Ron Griffin of Sparrow Records made this point: "A record contract and a recording are not the point of your ministry. It only falls in behind the wake of the ministry that God has blessed you with."[12]

The Heart of Worship

Despite the downside of some aspects of CCM, God has used many of the changes in music to His glory. CCM was born primarily from new believers who came to Christ from rock music, and it is touching the culture. The recent praise and worship music, however, is coming from the church. New hymns and choruses are energizing youth groups and churches across the nation, and youth have become part of one of the biggest revolutions in worship ever. Psalm 40:3 says, "He has put a new song in my mouth—Praise to our God."

When worship focuses on giving of ourselves to God, our Lord blesses us with His presence. Across America, in rooms tucked away upstairs in local churches, in large arenas, and in CD players, young people are returning to a fresh, earnest passion for authentic worship. An obvious example of this in the college arena is a movement called Passion, which has released several praise and worship CDs. In 2000 in Memphis and in 2003 in Texas, Passion held major music festivals with tens of thousands in attendance. There is, of course, always the danger in such times of focusing on the experience of worship over the God we are called to worship. Still, there's something healthy, even exciting, about the new wave of worshipers in our day.

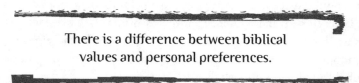

There is a difference between biblical
values and personal preferences.

Those of us who lead youth have the awesome responsibility of teaching them how to worship—as individuals, with their families, and corporately. So, in relation to music, what are some foundations today for corporate worship?

1. *Be biblical.* Youth may well get more theology from their songs than any source. It's fine to sing songs that touch the heart, but be sure to use songs that above all else teach biblical truth. In a year's time, can you say that youth have sung sound systematic theology?

2. *Be balanced.* The style of service matters, make no mistake, and music can add a lot to style. But style is secondary to substance. And often overlooked in the style over substance debate is spirit. I have been in many contemporary services, and some were spirit-filled while others had no life, just fluff. I've also been in many traditional services. Some were dead and some demonstrated great zeal for God. I personally prefer a more contemporary format, but that's simply my preference, and there is a difference between biblical values and personal preference.

3. *Be a part of the body.* Worship in such a way that speaks not only to the worshipers in your church, but that also connects them to the larger family of faith. In other words, it's fine to sing new songs, but also sing songs that maintain a heritage of the faith from generation to generation. Great hymns, for example, even when sung in a new way, do two things: first, they teach doctrine; second, they tie us to the best of the past. Dead tradition is a bad

thing; maintaining a biblical heritage, however, is a good thing. When your students go to college, they should find a church with some songs they know.

4. *Be a blessing more than being blessed.* Many think the purpose of coming to a worship service is to be blessed, and music can, indeed, offer a blessing. But the primary meaning of worship is to ascribe value, or worth, to another. So worship should focus more on being a blessing to God than on receiving blessings from Him. Enough narcissism is in the church now. Teach youth to offer themselves to God as living sacrifices.

Expository Worship: A New, Biblical Approach

"Add without subtracting" defines my attitude toward change. Change that can be done without jettisoning vital truths or approaches works best. The new movement in corporate worship has infused fresh life into thousands. But how can we, as youth leaders, encourage that new life, add new songs, and increase focus on God and His truth?

Trent Eayrs, a student of mine from South Africa, has a passion for true worship. He and a team of students have traveled with me for years, and during that time Trent has given much thought on how to lead corporate worship. Now doing just that at a vibrant church plant in our area, Trent conducts true, God-centered worship in both an itinerant ministry and in weekly services for a home congregation.

Trent has developed an approach he calls "expository worship." When he leads a group of people in public worship, the focus is not the songs but a text of Scripture. During expository worship, just as many songs are sung as in experienced-centered worship, and they're sung just as passionately. The difference is, the Bible becomes the guide for this time of worship, building a foundation that leads to the climax, the preaching of the Word.

In this approach the leader spends most of his time in the Scripture, allowing the text to determine the songs he selects. Passages are read, and the leader briefly comments on the passage, making the connection of song to text. The songs, then, become a melodic commentary on the text. Here's an example from the familiar passage in Isaiah 6. This passage is often used as a worship model, as it says much about worship, obedience, and missions.[13]

> In the year that king Uzziah died, I saw the Lord sitting on a throne, high and lifted up, and the train of His robe filled the temple. Above it stood seraphim; each one had six wings: with two he covered his face, with two he covered his feet, and with two he flew. And one cried to another and said:
>
> *"Holy, holy, holy is the Lord of hosts;*
> *The whole earth is full of His glory!"*
>
> And the posts of the door were shaken by the voice of him who cried out, and the house was filled with smoke.
>
> —Isaiah 6:1–4

Leader: "Isaiah's worship experience began with a vision of who God is. Let us take time today to acknowledge our God as Holy."
Songs related to this passage might include

- "Open the Eyes of My Heart"
- "Holy Holy Holy" (Heber)
- "We Fall Down"

> So I said:
>
> *"Woe is me, for I am undone!*
> *Because I am a man of unclean lips,*
> *And I dwell in the midst of a people of unclean lips;*
> *For my eyes have seen the King,*
> *The Lord of hosts."*
>
> —Isaiah 6:5

Leader: "Catching a glimpse of God's holiness highlights how sinful we are and how much we need God's presence."

Songs:

- "Give Us Clean Hands"
- "Break Our Hearts"
- "Come Thou Fount"
- "Hungry"

Then one of the seraphim flew to me, having in his hand a live coal which he had taken with the tongs from the altar. And he touched my mouth with it, and said:

> *"Behold, this has touched your lips;*
> *Your iniquity is taken away,*
> *And your sin purged."*
> —Isaiah 6:6–7

Leader: "There is a solution for our human condition—atonement. God provided a means for Isaiah to have his sin purged, a beautiful picture of what Christ has done for us."
Songs:

- "When I Survey/Wonderful Cross"
- "Once Again"
- "Here I Am to Worship"

Also I heard the voice of the Lord, saying:

> *"Whom shall I send,*
> *And who will go for Us?"*

Then I said, "Here am I! Send me."
> —Isaiah 6:8

Leader: "The end result of Isaiah's worship experience was a call to serve the Lord. As worshipers we too are called to be missionaries, so let's commit to follow hard after Him."

Songs:

- "Pure and Holy Passion"
- "Holiness"

Trent adds this reminder for those leading in this critical time: "An encounter with the holiness of God should be the wish of any true worshiper and therefore also the desire of the lead worshiper. God is the One we worship, so what better way to approach Him than on His terms? God does reveal Himself 'generally' to all individuals on the globe but 'specially' to those who know Him and have His Word. The terms are clear: let us, as lead worshipers, be broken over God's holy requirement for the worshiper, and thereafter use the same Scriptures to lead His children."

One vital emphasis Trent makes in corporate worship is that worship in spirit and truth inevitably leads to missions and evangelism. When we encounter God, we have to tell someone.

Here's another example from the New Testament:

> Now Peter and John went up together to the temple at the hour of prayer, the ninth hour. And a certain man lame from his mother's womb was carried, whom they laid daily at the gate of the temple which is called Beautiful, to ask alms from those who entered the temple.
>
> —Acts 3:1–2

Leader: "Do you remember a time when you were unable to worship with everybody else because of sin that crippled you? Consider the miracle of your testimony as we sing."

Songs:

- "Better Is One Day"
- "Amazing Grace" (Newton)
- "Forever"

> Who, seeing Peter and John about to go into the temple, asked for alms. And fixing his eyes on him, with John, Peter said,

"Look at us." So he gave them his attention, expecting to receive something from them.

—Acts 3:3–5

Leader: "An expectant heart of faith is required as we approach our Lord today in worship."
Songs:

- "In the Secret"
- "I Need Thee Every Hour" (Hawks)
- "Enough"

Then Peter said, "Silver and gold I do not have, but what I do have I give you: In the name of Jesus Christ of Nazareth, rise up and walk."

—Acts 3:6

Leader: "Have you considered the value of the name, Jesus Christ? He is Savior, Redeemer, Prince of Peace. . . ." (List names from songs chosen.)
Songs:

- "Prince of Peace (You Are Holy)"
- "In Christ Alone"
- "No Other Name"
- "Before the Throne of God Above" (PDI)
- "You Are My King (I'm Forgiven)"

And he took him by the right hand and lifted him up, and immediately his feet and ankle bones received strength. So he, leaping up, stood and walked and entered the temple with them—walking, leaping, and praising God. And all the people saw him walking and praising God.

—Acts 3:7–9

Leader: "Traditional, pious, religious worship is interrupted by joyful shouts and loud cries of praise as the beggar from outside responds to his physical and spiritual healing. Let us follow his example and respond in praise for the new life we have received."

Songs:

- "Come Thou Fount of Every Blessing"
- "Agnus Dei"
- "Praise the Lord! Ye Heavens, Adore Him"
- "Hear Our Praises" (Hillsongs)

> Then they knew that it was he who sat begging alms at the Beautiful Gate of the temple, and they were filled with wonder and amazement at what had happened to him.
>
> —Acts 3:10

Leader: "May this be true of those who see us. May the peoples be filled with wonder and amazement at what God has done in us."

Songs:

- "Everything That Has Breath"
- "Shout to the North"
- "Better Is One Day"

Certain themes should be consistent in our worship. Trent defines worship as ascribing worth to God. This is appropriate, and we should never lose sight of God—not man—being the focus. Worship involves meeting with God and, because our response to God matters as well, leaving that encounter changed. Hence, our worship should be Christ-centered while including an element of motivation for missions and evangelism. Thus there are generally two types of songs: some that allow the worshiper to respond to God and others that we sing to each other as a battle cry to motivate us in our missionary task.

A Generation of Leadership

As has been shown, one of the most effective ways to reach and teach this generation is through praise and worship music combined with biblical, relevant preaching. It's been shown, too, that God is moving in some extraordinary ways throughout the fabric of this teen culture, and worship has become a vital part of the Christian young person's experience. It's not uncommon to find teens involved in worship gatherings of up to two hours long. The unrushed atmosphere spent seeking and waiting upon God allows these worshipers to heartily confess their sin to God, as well as drink in a sense of His forgiveness, grace, and mercy. Joy and enthusiasm draw young people together.

Read Psalm 24:1–5. What kind of worshiper does God seek? Someone with clean hands, a pure heart. When you go to public worship on Sunday, or in your youth meetings, do you take time to prepare your heart to encounter God? Here are three practical tips to make worship more meaningful. First, public worship comes from private worship. The more time you spend alone with God, the more authentic public worship becomes. Second, remember that worship is not primarily about you, it's about Him. Keep your focus on Him, and concentrate on honoring Him. Finally, remember this whenever you worship: the more honest you are with God, the more real He will be to you. Open your heart to Him, and experience the mighty presence of God.

God is seeking true worshipers. Read John 4. He does not *need* worship. He *does* seek those who will worship Him. With them, no matter their age, He can touch the world.

What did God do in the first century when He said, "I want one man to set the course for the early church"? He didn't pick Peter, James, and John, although He used them. He didn't pick any of the first twelve disciples. Instead, he found the most radical, fanatical man in the ancient Near East, Saul of Tarsus. And what was Saul doing? He was persecuting Christians but, after Saul met Jesus, God used him to lead the church. Why? I believe it was because he was the most passionate person anywhere. God just turned Saul's passion to Himself. .

When Saul, soon known as Paul, began to worship the living God, he touched the world. Once Paul was involved in ministry, people got tired of him and said, "Paul, we're going to kill you." Paul said, "Cool." He said, "To die is gain; absence from the body is presence with the Lord." They said, "We're going to make you happy, Paul, we'll let you live." He said, "Groovy. Go ahead and let me live, I just want to preach. I'm not ashamed of the gospel." They said, "This is no good. I'll tell you what we'll do; we'll make you suffer." Paul said, "I know that the sufferings in this life are not worthy to be compared with the glory I'll see." These are not the attitudes of a lukewarm Christian; they're the attitudes of a fanatic.

Paul liked to worship and his worship led him to witness. That's what happens when one encounters Jesus. When Jesus' followers met Him after the resurrection, they worshiped (Matt. 28:16–20), and immediately He gave them the Great Commission—to witness. Worship led to witness in the life of Isaiah (Isa. 6), in the woman at the well (John 4), and in the early church (Acts 2:42–47).

If you truly worship God—not an experience, but God—it will cost you. If you stand for Jesus, it will cost you. But if you become a spiritual wimp who just serves Jesus when it's safe, it will cost you far more. You are not neutral—you're either nudging people around you toward Jesus, or you are nudging people toward hell.

God Is Looking for Worshipers

When I was fifteen years old I really sold out to God. I was saved when I was eleven, but at fifteen I said, "God, I want to serve You with my whole life. Sometimes I don't even know what worshiping You means, but I want to find out."

What I found out was that when you trust God, He will test you. I played football in high school. We were a part of the P Club for our school team. We had an athletic initiation program for a week. A bunch of non-Christians were on my football team. One big guy named Victor called two of us and said, "Alvin, curse!" (Remember—I had just two weeks before said, "God, I want to give You my life.") I immediately said, "No way." And I thought, "He's going to kill me." He wasn't ready for that response. Neither my friend Joel nor I would curse, so he brought us before the whole football team, and for about fifteen minutes they just mocked us and made fun of us. I wasn't feeling particularly spiritual at that moment!

But, in part because that awful experience, Joel and I decided to do something. We heard about a group called Fellowship of Christian Athletes, and so we started one. We began to meet regularly. Why? To *fellowship?* No, to *worship.* Two years later, the most influential clubs in our high school were the Fellowship of Christian Athletes and a Christian club we'd also started.

Our public high school sponsored a Christian youth retreat. We saw people's lives changed and it touched our whole school. Several from my high school and my senior class entered the ministry and are in the ministry now. We had no idea the impact we were going to have—we just wanted to learn how to worship God.

A Romanian pastor who faced tremendous persecution by Communists in his country observed that American Christianity speaks much of commitment, but little of surrender. Yet Romans 12:1–2 focuses on surrendering our lives, not just adding Jesus to our little list of commitments. This pastor distinguished between commitment and surrender with a simple illustration. Imagine that you have a sheet of paper and a pen. That sheet of paper represents your life. A person who *commits* to follow Jesus writes down what he will do for Jesus—how much money he will spend, how much time he will give, and so on—and sign at the bottom, offering the sheet to the Lord.

Handing a written list over to the Lord may sound spiritual, but it actually means we call the shots for our life. In contrast, a person *surrendered* to the Lord will sign the bottom of the sheet while it's blank, and then hand the sheet and the pen to Jesus, saying, "Lord, whatever You put on that sheet I will do." Worship means surrendering all we are to all He is, to bring glory to His name.

Remember those twelve spies who were sent out by Moses? Ten of them came back with a negative report. They brought down a nation—a whole generation missed the Promised Land because ten people failed to surrender all the power of their God. Worship is *that* important.

Chapter Eleven

Advice to Parents

It's Time to Grow Up

Hear, O Israel: The LORD our God, the LORD is one! You shall love the LORD your God with all your heart, with all your soul, and with all your strength.

And these words which I command you today shall be in your heart. You shall teach them diligently to your children, and shall talk of them when you sit in your house, when you walk by the way, when you lie down, and when you rise up. You shall bind them as a sign on your hand, and they shall be as frontlets between your eyes. You shall write them on the doorposts of your house and on your gates.

—Deuteronomy 6:4–9

Does this family sound familiar?

It has been twelve days since Mom, Dad, Erich, Janey, and Melissa Morgan had a meal together. No, Dad isn't out of town, and no one is angry. They didn't plan it this way, but they figure that is just the way life is today.

You see, Erich's bus leaves for high school at 7:05 A.M. Janey leaves for middle school at 7:40. Mom takes Melissa to elementary school at 8:45 A.M., and then she's off to work. She works 3/4 time so she can be with the children—but in reality, the only time she is "with" the children is when she's in the van. She feels more like a taxi driver than a mom.

Janey, one of the top acrobatic and jazz dancers in her troupe, has advanced dance class after school on Monday, Tuesday, and

Thursday until 6:00 P.M. (with an occasional Saturday morning rehearsal). Erich's high school basketball team, off to a two and seven start, is practicing overtime every day after school except on days when there are games. Melissa wants to be a dancer like Janey, so she practices with the beginner group, as soon as Janey's class is over.

Monday night is church visitation. Wednesday night there are church activities. Sunday night is church, too, of course. Almost every Friday or Saturday night at least one of the children is spending the night with a friend. And Saturday is lawn day, basketball games, dance performances . . . the list is endless. Mom is taking a computer course on Tuesday evenings. Some of Dad's clients insist on dinner meetings. There seem to be two or three a week.

Perhaps you recognize this family. Stretched, stressed, and losing touch with each other. This family is easy to find. It lives in your neighborhood, on your block, maybe in your house. . . . [But], you don't want to raise your family like the Morgans.[1]

The excerpt above is from *Family to Family* by Victor Lee and Jerry Pipes, and it illustrates a realistic depiction of a churched family in America. If we're to raise a generation to serve God, changing this picture is critical. Why? Because the greatest impact in the life of youth is not made by their peers; the greatest impact in the life of youth is made by adults, and especially by parents. That's why, too, in the future, effective youth ministers will—instead of spending 90 percent of their time with students—spend perhaps a third of their time with the students, a third of the time with parents and other significant adults, and a third of the time with all of them together. This will be a radical change for most youth ministers, but one that will move youth to change the world for God.

Today's Parents Want to Get It Right

Youth pastors consistently complain that the biggest hindrance to raising the bar in youth ministry is oftentimes parents. Many parents don't think of the long-term implications of a youth ministry that's based on silliness, yet it's the parents who cry the loudest when their children aren't having "fun." American youth have parents who grew up when being a parent too often meant being a "buddy" to children. The failure of parenting, and of marriages for that matter, has had a serious, negative impact on millions of youth. But if many of the problems facing youth begin with parents, the solution can begin there as well. And many children want their parents to make that change.

> Here the Millennials are indeed special, since they are demonstrably reversing a wide array of negative youth trends, from crime to profanity to sex to test scores that have prevailed in America for nearly half a century. In other words, Millennials are reversing the long-term direction of change—the delta of history. Today's kids are doing this so dramatically that, as a group, they are behaving better than their parents did as kids—and better than many or their parents (or leaders) behave even now, as adults.[2]

Parents, how do you see youth ministry? Do you think that youth ministry should primarily provide activities for your children? If so, please take a day off work and, instead, take your child to a theme park yourself. Over the past several years my work with youth and youth ministers has led me to a clear conviction: parents of youth need to rediscover the biblical teaching of Deuteronomy 6:4–9. According to God's Word, the primary place of spiritual training is not the church but the home! It's true that youth ministry can have a strong role in helping youth from lost families connect with both the church and other adults. But the very best youth ministry should be nothing more for *Christian* families than an aid to them, providing a supporting, not a leading, role.

The good news is that parents as a group over the past decade have increasingly shown a growing interest in getting it right with their children. And increasingly youth pastors focus on the long-term impact of the church's ministry to teens. Mark DeVries, a youth pastor, decided to take a radical approach: "I was, and still am, committed to taking whatever steps are necessary to accomplish the intended purpose of the student ministry of our church: to lead young people toward Christian adulthood." He adds, "In a youth culture undergirded by stable families and many available adults, the old model of youth ministries (isolating youth from the world of adults for an hour or two) worked fine. But in the current environment . . . the old model for youth ministry is no longer capable of carrying young people to Christian maturity."[3]

DeVries states further, "But at the same time [that] our culture seems to be losing our moorings about what a healthy family is, there is an unprecedented interest among Christian parents to learn to be faithful and effective in helping their children grow as Christians. The mid '90s growth of the Promise Keepers Movement among Christian fathers has been nothing short of amazing. And some of the best-selling Christian books have directed Christian parents . . . to break the old, negative patterns they grew up with."[4]

- Only 34 percent of America's families eat one meal together each day.
- The average father spends eight to ten minutes a day with his children including meal and television times.
- Only 12 percent of America's families pray together.
- The average couple spends only four minutes of uninterrupted time together a day.[5]

DeVries says, "In almost twenty years in working with teenagers, I have never seen this sort of genuine concern and determination of Christian parents that we are seeing today. Perhaps now more than ever, parents want to join us as partners in ministry and are simply waiting to be asked." Children, he observes, also want a strong relationship with their parents. "Another reason for drawing on the natural power of families at this particular time in our culture is that kids want to have better relationships with their parents and spend more time with them. When one in four teenagers indicated that they have never had a meaningful conversation with their fathers, is it any wonder that 76 percent of teenagers surveyed in *USA Today* actually want their parents to spend more time with them? The stereotype of teenagers who want nothing more than to avoid their parents' input and influence is simply not consistent with the research of families today."[6]

Devries' observations parallel my research. As I've spoken to thousands of teens and their families over the past few years, I've been deluged with parents who want to do the right thing. Deuteronomy 6:4–9 offers timeless guidance for parents, but the way most Christian parents try to raise their children diverges radically from this biblical passage. Today, even the best-intentioned parents spend their time dealing with *behavior*, when what they should focus on is *belief*.

Deuteronomy 6:4–5, one of the most quoted passages in the Bible, begins with a statement of belief: *God is one*. Period. End of discussion. Are we teaching this fact to our children—that everything in life comes under the authority of the one, great, awesome, loving holy God? The passage goes on to say that parents are to *teach* truth to their children. How? By saying it and by living it—when you walk in the way, when you sit in your house, when you rise. In other words, Christianity lived only on Sundays will never change the world for your children or others.

When I speak I often ask audiences how many grew up in a Christian home, and the response is normally 80 to 90 percent. But the culture has changed. Over the past generation, pluralism, relativism, and a litany of moral concerns from homosexuality to abortion have altered the cultural landscape. We cannot raise our children the way we were raised. We as parents must raise the bar in our Christian living!

The word *we* refers to both moms *and* dads. Robert Lewis makes this stirring, and accurate, observation: a cultural revolution has begun. What college students were to the 1960s, what women were to the 1970s, and what yuppies were to the 1980s, dads may be to the 1990s and beyond. Fathers are coming home. And it's not just within the ranks of evangelical Christianity. The revolution transcends religious, racial, and ethnic boundaries.[7]

Do youth observe their parents having daily devotions? Do parents pray with their youth? A survey by Lifeway Christian Resources found 92 percent of Southern Baptist homes have no devotional times during the year. Praying with their youth needs to be elevated as one of the highest priorities in the home. Strong parent ministry is a necessary component if we are going to win this generation to Christ. Training parents to share the gospel with youth must be an integral part of youth ministry.[8]

Here are a few practical tips to help move your family to a Deuteronomy 6 model:

1. Remember this basic principle of time management: *If you don't control your time, someone else will.* Michelle and I were older than our peers when we had kids, so we observed many parents who had children older than ours. So many families were exhausted, going from activity to activity. So, while our kids were still small, we decided that we wouldn't do activities such as sports year-round. Our kids are both great athletes, and I'm a *huge* supporter of sports as a means to teach about life. But we decided our family mattered more than sports. So we take one sports "season" off a year. You can't implement the lived-out faith of Deuteronomy 6 when you're exhausted from behaving more like taxi drivers than parents. We tried to set the standard early that Mom and Dad, not activities, would set the calendar.

2. A second factor of time management, *Make time to do what is important*—like faithful attendance in worship. Like family times of devotion. Like times to get away as a family. Like regular family nights and meals together.

3. *Men, give your wife and kids the very best of your discretionary time.* We live incredibly busy lives. I travel a lot, but my kids know I'd rather be home than on the road. Why? Because I *would* rather be at home

than on the road! You may work an eight-to-five job and never go anywhere, but if you don't want to be home, your kids will know it.

4. *Everyday, do something in your children's world.* I'm a professor at a fast-growing, incredibly hectic seminary. I write nearly a book a year, preach in forty-plus churches annually, and on and on. But every week, several days a week, I help my grade-school daughter with her homework. Do I do it because I love it? No, as a professor, at the end of the day I'd rather do something else than more schoolwork. But I do it because it is important to Hannah. And because helping with homework is what a parent (I did *not* say just a mom) should do. As I write this paragraph, I'm about to go and rebound for Josh's free throws, because spending time in a child's world each day is critical.

5. *Discover what your kids love to do, and regularly do it with them.* That shows your kids that they matter to you. Take your daughter roller skating. Shoot hoops with your son. It's okay if you're pitiful at it; if your child loves doing it, spend time doing it with your child.

I broke my hip a few years ago and had a hip replacement. I sat and wept bitterly the morning I realized I could never play tackle football with my son as he grew older. It tore me apart! But we all decided to focus on what I can do, and neither of my children has ever complained about what I can't do. I'm simply as available as possible to do what I can with them.

Showing your kids that you care can be done in very practical ways in the home. Sit at the foot of the bed longer. Eat meals together. Go to ball games. Sacrifice for them. Discipline them. And, as mentioned, find out what's important to them and do it with them. Do you even know what things are most important to your children? If not, put this book down and go find out. Do it now, especially if your children are young, because if you wait until they're seventeen, you've missed your window of opportunity.

The Desire of Youth

"If you turn your back on God, will He ever let you come back?" I had just finished my conference in Green Lake, Wisconsin, when a young lady asked me that question. I could see pain in her eyes, far too much pain for a thirteen-year-old to bear.

I asked her name, and she said, "Karen." I turned to Romans 8 and showed Karen what the Bible says—that nothing can separate us from the love of God. But Karen needed more than a simple affirmation. There was so much hurt on her face that I asked her to sit down and talk to me. Then she asked me, "Do you believe what you're telling people?" The reason some people don't believe our message is because they're not sure whether *we* believe it! "Yes, I do," I replied.

She looked at me and, with bitterness in her voice, said, "My dad is a pastor. He talks like you do. He says things about God like you do. But he doesn't live it at home." She described the hypocrisy of her father, and my heart broke for her. She said she lived in a little "hick" town in the middle of nowhere. She told me how her mom and dad loved her older brother, but not her. She seemed to be a nuisance, an embarrassment. She told me she had become a Satanist, and she cursed her father.

I asked her if Satan had made her life any better (this was not my first encounter with a Satanist wanna-be). Surprised by the question, she admitted nothing in Satanism had helped her hurt, and admitted it was simply a means to escape. Her eyes teared up, revealing her hopelessness, yet confirming much of the positive things I'd said about her generation. She just couldn't see those things happening in her life.

Few times in my life have I been more brokenhearted. I thought of my son, at the time also thirteen. I thought of my precious daughter, Hannah, and did not want to imagine her in such a situation. I told Karen lots of things, but mostly I just let her vent. She let me pray with her, and when I started to leave, I asked her if I could give her a hug. I put my arm around her shoulder, and she hugged me so hard. I don't think she was getting many hugs at this point in her life.

All youth of every generation loathe hypocrisy. But this generation has an extremely low hypocrisy threshold. We'll never touch this generation if we fail to live what we preach. One more thing I learned from Karen. Only thirteen, she was very bright. She could smell a rat a mile away. She had apparently met a few. If we use ministry to teens for any other reason than to bring them to Jesus, they will know.

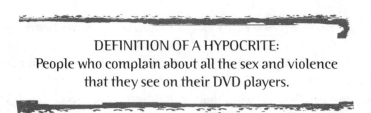

DEFINITION OF A HYPOCRITE:
People who complain about all the sex and violence
that they see on their DVD players.

Your kids want you in their lives. But if years of communication problems have built up walls, it will take time to tear them down. And if you think your teenager loathes the very thought of being around you, think again. I'm reminded of the mom who asked me to explain her daughter's behavior. The daughter had asked her mom to be an adult leader at a youth retreat, and she agreed. But once they got to the retreat, the daughter seemed to want to have nothing to do with her mom. Why? Because her daughter wanted her around, but at the same time she wanted some space. "Family is a big deal to teenagers, regardless of how they act or what they say," Barna observed. "It is the rare teenager who believes he or she can lead a fulfilling life without receiving complete acceptance and support from his or her family." Barna discovered, in fact, that "in spite of the seemingly endless negative coverage in the media about the state of the family these days, most teens are proud of their family. Nine out of 10 (90 percent) consider their family to be 'healthy and functional.' This is an extraordinarily high figure given that one-third of the teens interviewed are living in either a 'blended' or 'broken' home—i.e., a home situation in which they are not living with both of their natural parents."[9]

Teenagers seek the respect of their parents. Teenagers wish their parents would be more trusting that their teens were capable of making good decisions. They wish, too, that their parents would better understand the strengths of teens. Barna also learned that, in surveys, youth scored their parents low on follow through on commitments. Teens notice when parents don't keep their promises. Still, Barna's research shows that the people the teens spend the most time with—their friends—were the least likely to give them a sense of peace. Rather, the people that gave them the most sense of peace were their parents.[10]

Ruth Bell Graham, the wife of Billy Graham, is said to have given this advice to parents: When your children are young, teach them; when they're older, listen to them. Today, however, youth spend an average of three and one-half hours alone each day, and 63 percent of youth live in homes where both parents work. Who, then, is teaching and listening to these kids? As Josh McDowell puts it, "When young people don't feel that you identify with them, they are less likely to stay connected emotionally to you."[11]

In his book *The Disconnected Generation*, McDowell offers six areas where parents can and must connect with their children:

- **Affirmation**—giving youth a sense of authenticity
- **Acceptance**—giving youth a sense of security
- **Appreciation**—giving youth a sense of significance
- **Affection**—giving youth a sense of lovability
- **Availability**—giving youth a sense of importance
- **Accountability**—giving youth a sense of responsibility

What Can a Church Do?

If the parents are believers, the primary place of spiritual nurture and training for children should be the home, with the church accenting and enhancing this teaching. If Christian parents assumed spiritual responsibility for their children, more church resources could be focused on assisting youth from non-Christian homes. These youth need huge amounts of teaching, love, and encouragement.

How selfish it would be, then, for even parents who are most active in the church to expect youth ministry to revolve around their children! Yet I see this "church is a hotel for saints, not a hospital for sinners" mentality all too often.

Still, churches can and do teach biblical principles on raising children to adulthood. For years I've asked my students how many of them have been members of a church that featured a sermon series on the home or sponsored a parenting conference. Most have. Shouldn't churches also teach parents how to lead their children to Christ? When I ask my students, though, how many of them have heard, in the course of the sermons or conferences, any teaching on how parents can lead their children to Christ, students have almost never responded in the positive to that question. Nothing should be more important to a Christian parent than to see his or her child come to Christ, yet the church seldom, if ever, teaches parents how to evangelize their own children. Maybe our sermons and conferences on parenting are missing the point.

Parents, it's time for us to come back to the priority of the Christian home. Remember what Kristin said at the beginning of this book? "Tell [teachers who work with youth that] we know how to be teenagers. We want them to show us how to be adults."

A student I know grew up in church. His parents were quite active in church activities but, by middle school, the boy was out of control. Why? The answer is simple. His dad would not discipline him and had no time for him. Although the family was active in church, parenting was apparently off the radar screen. When things got really bad, the student was sent to a boot camp to learn discipline. He came back changed and, in fact, he didn't want to leave the camp and go home. He'd found what he was missing—loving, but firm, discipline.

Nearly everyone knows that today's youth culture is filled with images and words that most adults find offensive. But here's what hardly anyone knows: Most kids find them offensive, too. In a 1998 survey of high-achieving high school students, 36 percent said they were "very" or "extremely" offended by sexual activity in the media—and another 26 percent said they were "moderately" offended. This is true for all ethnic groups. In an outlandish aspect of today's culture-war charades, many adults are shocked when they hear fifteen-year-olds spew back a few artifacts of a pop culture that includes South Park dialogue, Duke Nukem sound effects, and Limp Bizkit lyrics. Yet few adults express any particular shock at the thirty-year-olds who write it, the fifty-year-olds who produce it, or the seventy-year-olds whose portfolios profit by it.[12]

Evaluate How Adults See Youth

Many parents view the teen years as no more than a horrible period they must somehow suffer through. Enough of this. Yes, they are challenging years. Yes, they take much work and prayer. But they are also full of opportunities to guide our children into the adult world.

Parents, how do you see your children? I agree with David Black, who argues that parents are to expect the best, not the worst, from their children. Assuming they will turn out badly, rearing them to focus incessantly on what could go wrong with their lives, can become a self-fulfilling prophecy. "If we expect them to act like irresponsible children, they will," Black states. "On the other hand, if we expect them to act like responsible adults, as people did for thousands of years, they will."[13]

Barna's research found the following: "While adults, especially in the media, have a tendency to refer to teenagers as pessimistic, 'slackers' and self absorbed, teens resent such depictions."[14] Seven adjectives describing teens were chosen to show what teens believed adults thought of them. Five of the seven are negative: lazy, rude, sloppy, dishonest, and violent. The two positive ones were friendly and intelligent. The adults rated teenagers high on all those. "Naturally, few teens view themselves or their generation in such negative terms," Barna observed. "However, such a projection helps to explain why teens struggle with taking directions from, or being educated by, adults: They do not believe that adults respect, understand them or give the freedom and creative license that they desire."[15]

Certainly teenagers with their hormonal changes and their developing minds have a rebellious streak in them—no doubt about it. But parents inadvertently often encourage that rebellious streak by treating teenagers like fourth graders. Perhaps we should try, instead, respecting them and listening to them. I'm weary of hearing youth tell me, as just happened last week at a church, that they feel adults consider youth to be a nuisance in the church.

Hi, Dr. Reid:

Today when I had mentioned God twice (because I want to start a Bible study, and because I wanted to get Rob into something dealing with "religion") my parents said that they have become really concerned about me. They think I'm becoming obsessed with religion, and religion is a private matter, and a bunch of other stuff. I want so much to be able to live for Jesus without hiding it. . . . I know that [my parents' doubts are] only making me stronger, but it still hurts. I think what hurts the most is that I love my parents . . . and I'm so scared that once I'm able to live for Jesus (after high school, when I'm sort of on my own) . . . maybe that they won't approve of me. . . . I don't know. They don't think I'm old enough to make decisions about religion yet. I'm not really sure when they think I will be. . . . I'm kind of guessing it will be when I get out of high school.

Pam

Pam represents many youth today who have a greater spiritual hunger than their parents, and whose parents hold back their spiritual growth. Today the trend is to raise kids with virtual parents, who use cell phones and beepers as a leash. Ostensibly the cell phones are for the safety of the students but, in effect, it gives the parents another justification to get the kids out of their hair.

> Good-bye to body-piercing, green hair, grunge music and the deliberately uncouth look. Hello to kids who look up to their parents and think bowling is fun.[16]

Clearly, Pam's parents do not envision her as a leader in church. As a teen I was in a church that involved the youth every Sunday night in choir. As a group we had leadership, and one Sunday a year we had youth day. But even then we had very few opportunities to develop leadership skills. The church required that a youth serve on the pastor search committee. But youth need more; they need to be allowed to develop leadership skills while young.

Besides at home and in church, another place that youth should be learning these skills is in school. I'm a radical on education, and I'm not alone. Specialists in various fields are looking at the needs of adolescents and asking whether the nation's high schools are meeting them. Many experts believe that by not challenging teenagers' considerable powers—which are often equal to those of adults—and by not building on their desire to connect with the adult world, high schools all too often place students in a motivational vacuum. Combine that with conditions at odds with the teenage body—early start times, too little sleep, too much seat time—and educators on the front lines are confronted with a formidable challenge. The result is that too many schools are losing too many students—if not in body, then in mind and spirit.

Many researchers make the point that by age fifteen or so, youth are in many ways the physical and mental equals—even superiors—of adults. Older teenagers are at their lifetime peak for such characteristics as speed, reaction time, and memory. They are also generally more daring than adults. Leon Botstein—president of Bard College in Annandale-on-Hudson, New York, and a critic of American high schools—argues that recent phenomena in human biology play a role in teenagers' dissatisfaction with high school. Today's teenagers, Botstein says, typically reach puberty two or three years earlier than their counterparts at the beginning of the twentieth century and so, by the end of high school, have had the physical hallmarks of adult men and women for several years.[17]

Considering, then, the ambitions, the physical, mental, and spiritual capabilities of youth, doesn't it seem that the teen years are the ideal time to teach these kids to be leaders?

The Place of Youth Ministry: Zookeepers or Role Models?

I spoke at a youth rally at a megachurch that has hundreds of students in attendance. The youth pastor, a twenty-something guy with two rings in his ears who was trying way too hard to look cool, came up and introduced himself to me, "I'm the zookeeper." I bit my tongue, but my thought was, "If you treat teens like animals, you need a zookeeper!"

I was introduced as an old guy, which is no problem, but even the youth pastor who introduced me seemed shocked, almost skeptical, that a forty-something could communicate to teens. Such a false assumption does not encourage youth to plan far ahead for a life of service to God. I thank God for the youth pastor at our church; he's committed to raising the bar. Nonetheless, I am my son's *main* youth minister.

Who, though, will minister to youth whose families are nonbelievers? While the role of youth ministry is to give biblical emphasis for strengthening Christian families in the church, a further role is to evangelize lost families of youth who attend. How many youth pastors or ministries would boast that in a given year scores of youth from unchurched homes attend their church, but those same ministers give virtually no attention to reaching those parents? What could be more important to the future of those youth than to see their parents come to Christ?

In terms of strengthening Christian families, I'm not advocating the position that a twenty-three-year-old youth pastor should teach parents how to raise their teens. But that pastor can show youth how to walk with God, can teach the Word, and can provide resources—such as strong Christian families as examples—to aid other families.

Involve Significant Adults

What more vital role could older adults have in the church than to take under their wing a student from an unsaved family? Multitudes of young people come from lost homes and may themselves be lost. We must challenge older adults to pour their lives into such young adults. I recently read of a man in his sixties who retired and decided to become the grandfather at the local high school. He volunteered for everything possible. A short time ago, he went to a basketball game. When he entered the gym, it was decorated in his honor. He and his wife received a standing ovation from the entire student body. A short, bald guy, whom you'd never find on the cover of a youth workers' magazine, he's not someone many would look at and say, "That's the guy I want doing youth ministry." But no youth pastor had earned the affection of the students like this retired gentleman.

> I preached on the home at a church in South
> Carolina. A layman came to me after the service in tears.
> "If I had been taught these principles thirty-five years
> ago, my daughter might not be a lesbian today." People
> want to be taught how to raise their kids.

Richard R. Dunn uses the acronym SOAP—Significant Other Adult Person—to refer to "those important mentors who can make all the difference in . . . maturation." How, though, do churched youth, as well as newly converted youth, connect with a SOAP if young people are continually funneled into youth programs? "Youth leaders in local churches must guard against developing youth ministries that are 'mini parachurches.' Parachurch leaders likewise face the challenge of connecting converts to local church fellowships." Dunn recognizes that failure to address these concerns can lead to two negative results: "First, in the present, students miss the rich spiritual heritage of intergenerational relationships in the body of Christ. Second, in the future, students lacking meaningful connections to the broader faith community often drop out of church following high school graduation."[18]

Youth pastors, then, have a formidable responsibility. Many criticize, with some justification, that many youth ministries today seem to be built on entertainment. But the truth is, whatever you're doing, if you see no change in your students over time, you're merely entertaining them, not mentoring them.

A seven-year-old went through his parents' devastating divorce. For months after the divorce he was wetting his pants. His father tried everything to correct the problem. He read books. He took his son to the doctor. He sent off for programs. Nothing worked. Finally, the father sat down with his son and asked, "What's going on? Babies do this."

The boy answered, "And their daddies hold them."

Children of all ages need adults. What if parents are AWOL? What about students in your church whose parents don't care about the things of God? Involving adults, whether parents or not, is vital to the development of youth in the church. DeVries hits the mark when he asks:

> Where do hurting students turn for their most significant long-term health? In her fascinating book, *Children of Fast Track Parents,* A. A. Brooks documents, "Studies of resiliency in children show time and again that consistent emotional support of at least one loving adult can help children overcome all sorts of chaos and deprivation." Urie Bronfrenbrenner's declaration, "Somebody's got to be crazy about the kid," points to the heart of family-based youth ministry. *Perhaps the best gift a youth ministry can give teenagers is not to impress them or attract them, but to ensure that each young person has an adult in the church who delights in him or her.* The church family becomes the family base."[19]

It is a sad fact of life that often the stronger the youth program in the church, and the more deeply the young people of the church identify with it, the weaker the chances are that those same young people will remain in the church when they grow too old for the youth program. Why? Because the youth program has become a substitute for participation in the church. . . . When the kids outgrow the youth program, they also outgrow what they have come to know of the church.[20]

As I type this I'm sitting in an airline terminal working on my laptop. A television is showing an NFL playoff game. I occasionally glance up at it while I listen to a praise and worship CD. At my side is my cell phone, which just rang—no, it vibrated. I even have a palm pilot in my pocket. I'm watching, listening, feeling. I just need to connect to the Internet and get an instant message going, and then I'll really be wired to the world.

We have so many ways to communicate. We've been blessed with technology like the world has never seen. But all the technology has failed to bring human beings closer together. Technology doesn't guarantee intimacy. It may, in fact, hinder intimacy due to the distraction it brings. People, especially young people, need intimacy in relationships.

Perhaps that explains why many youth organizations that were begun by older adults have failed. Barna notes, "Too few organizations have effectively rallied young people around the vision, a cause or purpose, that might ordinarily appeal to young adults: more often than not, those organizations are led by adults perceived to hold negative views about teens and young adults. Without a sense of acceptance and respect, young people are not prone to submitting themselves to the leadership of people or organizations who failed to embrace them as people."[21]

Acceptance and respect is the secret to Ron Luce and his Acquire the Fire Ministry. Thousands, sometimes tens of thousands, gather in huge arenas for an Acquire the Fire two-day event. Luce's vision is successful because he believes in young people, and he challenges them to do great things for God, like overseas missions projects.

The first institution God created was not the church. It was not government. It was the home. And the home lies at the very heart of the church's task today—helping parents to be leaders of their children, to raise their children to be champions for God.

Chapter Twelve

Meanwhile, Back at the Church

And He Himself gave some to be apostles, some prophets, some evangelists, and some pastors and teachers, for the equipping of the saints for the work of ministry, for the edifying of the body of Christ.
—Ephesians 4:11–12

Youth pastors, are you up for a change? If so, you're not alone. One of the greatest blessings I've had in the past three years is speaking to youth pastors and lay youth workers at camps and other settings. The Quest Camp, an excellent camp ministry of InQuest Ministries, is one such example. The following e-mail from a youth pastor at a Quest Camp represents dozens of similar e-mails and phone calls I've received from youth pastors:

Dr. Reid,

I attended the Quest Camp during 2002 and heard your presentation on "Raising the Bar." I just wanted to take the opportunity to thank you for your words of encouragement. For the last few years I have found that I am not "fitting in" inside the church setting of youth ministry as well as I used to. I wondered if God was changing the focus of my calling or if I was just way off base or losing my mind (my wife still thinks the latter is an option).

It just doesn't make sense to do [youth] ministry like most churches attempt to do it. I thought that I was an absolute idiot until I heard your words (that was meant as a compliment!).

You have, through your words of honest passion, changed our entire youth ministry as well as my focus and purpose for being a youth pastor. I have been in either full- or part-time youth pastor positions for the last eleven years or so. I am just now getting my much needed (formal) education. I say formal in that I believe I have attained very much education (and failure) in just "doing" ministry. There was a time when that seemed to work, but not now! I need to learn more theology in order to teach it more effectively! As Maxwell says, "You can't lead someone where you have never been."

In at least three years, I hope the students in my youth ministry are sending you an e-mail and thanking you for your words to me!

Thanks for pushing RELATIONSHIP over Religion to me, Dr. Reid! I will never forget our brief God-ordained encounter! Keep it real, and please pray for me and what God wants to do with my life.

Connected to Jesus,
Keith

I've had the honor of being in several churches where the hand of God moved in powerful revival. I've also spent years studying the history of awakenings, and have observed in history what I've witnessed personally: rare indeed is the church that experiences revival without the zeal of youth. But youth have often told me, "We don't feel we have a place in the church." Perhaps one reason, then, that so many churches have lost their fire for God is because they have pushed youth to the periphery of church life. Churches need it all—the zeal and energy of youth *and* the wisdom and maturity of older believers. How, though, can we bring students back into the church?

A Word to Pastors

I love pastors and have devoted my life to training them. But all too often pastors leave their youth pastors hanging out to dry. One very sharp and godly youth pastor led an effective ministry, but some young ladies in the group felt like they were being neglected by him. They started a vicious rumor, saying that he'd been inappropriate with them. Their parents were active and prominent in the church and of the conviction that youth ministry existed more to pacify churched youth than to reach the lost. They attacked the youth pastor, and the pastor would not stand by the youth pastor even though his ministry had been one of integrity from the first day. Ultimately the young ladies repented of their lies, but so much damage had been done by then, the youth pastor had to leave that ministry.

Pastors, if you call a youth pastor, support him. If he's a young man, mentor him. In the past, young men called to the ministry served as an apprentice to the pastor. Today that tradition is largely lost, although some pastors of larger churches have revived an intern ministry. Instead, most young men in the ministry begin as youth pastors. They still need a pastor to guide them, to teach them how to be youth *pastors,* not *youth* pastors. And they certainly need a pastor to support them. Don't hire a youth pastor just to get the youth ministry out of your hair or the parents off your back.

Youth pastors often complain that they're treated like second-class ministers, not quite up to the standard of "real" ministry. So they're patronized and too often not taken seriously. Youth pastors may, however, perpetuate such a mentality by their own behavior. I've spoken in about eight hundred churches in the past fifteen years, and many times a youth event was the reason. Youth pastors, compared to everyone else I deal with, are by far less likely to return calls, keep up with details, and have a general grasp of ministry. So if you're a youth pastor, it's an unfortunate reality that you may have to work harder to be taken seriously as a minister. Don't, however, make the task more difficult by being unable to manage a calendar or make a meeting on time. If you want to dress like a teenager, fine, but don't complain when adults treat you like one. If we're to raise the bar, it starts with us—the ones who are in authority over youth.

The Pastor and the Youth Pastor Are a Team

Youth pastor and a pastor—find ways to encourage one another, to build up each other's ministry in the church you both serve. Youth pastor, involve your pastor whenever possible with the youth. Ask him at least once or twice a year to speak to your students. One pastor, who had formerly spent years in youth ministry, shared a valuable lesson. After hiring a sharp youth pastor, he basically forgot about that whole area of his church. Then his youth pastor invited him to speak to the youth on a Wednesday night. Afterwards, the pastor was amazed at the number of e-mails he received from students in the church, and how they began to speak to him on Sundays. Young people often get the idea that they don't matter, and some pastors unintentionally give that impression.

Notice what Barna discovered about teens, church, and pastors.[1] Teens were given a list of eighteen factors related to church, and were asked to choose which were most important to them. The number one factor related to the people and their friendliness. The second related to the sermon quality and the theological beliefs of the church (two-thirds of teens consider that critical). Third was liking the pastor—not the youth pastor, but the *pastor*. Half of young people indicated that the pastor was important to them. Of interest, Barna found the least important factors were how far the church was from home, the length of the sermons, and the availability of small groups.

Models of Youth Ministry: Youth Ministry or Not?

Raising the Bar challenges the church to examine how we view youth, and to set a higher standard in the fundamental ways we minister to them and to their families. It is the intent of *Raising the Bar*, then, to encourage and challenge you to expect more from and offer more to youth.[2] *Raising the Bar* is not, however, a "how-to" book on the nuts and bolts of organizing a youth ministry nor an endorsement of any particular approach to student ministry (although I've identified ministries that, in my opinion, get it right). Rather, the challenge is, on the one hand, to focus on the big picture—the general philosophy of ministering to youth in the church today—and on the other hand to focus on the bottom line of witness, worship, Bible teaching, prayer, and theology.

Yet a major issue of contemporary youth ministry concerns its very existence. Numerous books, articles, and web sites have been written or launched examining the level to which a church should be involved in youth ministry. And segregation within our churches is, indeed, a thorny issue. In the Western church, the whole concept of youth ministry is being reevaluated, and with good reason. The failure of youth ministry to produce a generation of strong, young adult believers has created strong reactions. Some advocate the abolition of such segregation, and thus the elimination of youth ministry.[3]

It's beyond the scope of this book to address the issue of segregation versus integration. Rather, the purpose is to challenge the current system to a total reformation. As John Wesley's reforms and revival movement led to the beginning of the Methodist Church, we may be seeing in our day the beginning of a movement that will radically change how we see youth ministry.

Martin Luther had no idea what impact his Ninety-five Theses would have when he nailed them on the door at Wittenberg; he simply sought to debate issues of concern. History gives many examples of changes, of biblical renewals, that went far beyond the original vision. The multitudes of churches I've seen and the many students I teach clearly indicate that we can raise the bar for a new vision.

It's almost impossible to predict a movement of God, but I sure want to be in on it when it comes! It's obvious, then, that *Raising the Bar* argues for a reformation of youth ministry, not the abolition of it. It takes time, though, to implement major changes. As one youth pastor of a megachurch told me, "Alvin, if I told my church we should abolish ministry to youth the way we currently do it, they would only fire me and hire another youth pastor."

So segregation of youth in the church is acceptable—as long as three points are followed. *First,* those desiring to segregate the youth from the rest of the church should have a clear, biblically justifiable reason. The same should be true for separating women, or the choir, or men's groups, or others in any ongoing way. One could argue, for example, for a separate youth meeting for the purpose of evangelizing youth, or for the purpose of giving specific instruction to youth. If, on the other hand, you propose abolishing separate youth meetings, then you must be consistent and stop having women's meetings and so on, except for special times.

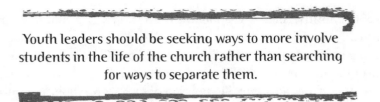

Youth leaders should be seeking ways to more involve students in the life of the church rather than searching for ways to separate them.

Second, limit segregation to those times when it's absolutely necessary. This can include a weekly meeting; however, youth pastors should constantly ask the question, "How can I involve youth more in the life of the whole church?" over, "How can I take the youth away from the life of the church?" One church had a sign on the youth room saying "Youth Room—Parents Not Allowed." While it was obviously tongue-in-cheek, the attitude of prohibiting parents is not a laughing matter. Youth need to learn, not how to follow a Pied Piper, but more biblical ecclesiology.

Some churches today have separate worship services on Sunday mornings for the youth. Splitting up our families at church is bad enough; can we really argue for youth services from the position of biblical ecclesiology? We must reexamine how we teach families to come together to church, separate, and then reunite on the way home. That's not an ideal to seek. Enough fragmentation of the family happens without the church contributing to it.

Third, even when you have times of segregation, make sure a significant number of mature adults are involved. Why? Because that's what youth want, more than we realize. And it's definitely what they need— the wisdom and maturity of older adults, and adults need the passion and zeal of younger adults. We need each other.

What, then, is the long-term answer to raise a generation who will change the world? There's a wide spectrum of opinion on the "to do youth ministry or not to do youth ministry" continuum. One extreme is to perpetuate the status quo: offer increasingly bigger and better games and events, creep closer and closer to the world. One church, in order to attract youth, even showed MTV videos each week. Such an approach will not change things for the better.

On the other extreme, churches can totally eliminate youth ministry and be built on family units. Biblical ecclesiology, however, teaches neither extreme separation *nor* a church model built on family units. The church is the body of Christ, not a family conference.

Youth ministers, if we move to a model of helping parents be the main youth ministers to their children, if we emphasize far less segregation, games, and so on, you might think doing so will work you out of a job. The issue, however, is not whether you have a job. If your concern is maintaining a position, please get out of the ministry now. I teach evangelism at a seminary, but if God moved in such a way and the church became so evangelistic that I wasn't needed to teach, I have enough faith in God to find me a place. It's not about us or our position. It is about *Him.*

I'm not ready to say, though, that youth ministry has no place. Youth ministry needs serious retooling, not abolishing—reforming not razing. Youth ministry is needed because families aren't raising the bar, parents often being the greatest hindrance to their own children becoming radicals for Jesus. So just as youth need more training in evangelism, parents need help in raising up a new generation. And youth pastors can play a vital role in both, especially when it comes to reaching and helping youth from non-Christian homes.[4]

Youth Ministry with a Purpose

Doug Fields, student minister at the Saddleback Valley Community Church in California, is candid in his book, *Purpose-Driven Youth Ministry (PDYM)*. He came to realize that building youth ministry on activities did not work: "I've been living with the weighty responsibility of developing a youth ministry that equips students, rather than a youth ministry that coordinates events. I don't want to direct programs; I want to disciple students."[5]

PDYM demonstrates how Fields moved to a purpose-driven model of ministry to students. Fields' book mirrors what his senior pastor, Rick Warren, said in his book *The Purpose-Driven Church.*[6] And that is as it should be. If you have a youth ministry whose purpose is distinct from that of the church, you're not a ministry of the church, you are a parachurch organization. The essential purpose of the church should not changed for, nor altered for, different groups within the church.

Nine components make up Fields' model:

1. *The power of God*—working through passionate leaders with pure hearts;
2. *Purpose*—discovering why your ministry exists and following it up with communication and leadership;
3. *Potential audience*—identifying which students are the target for the purposes;
4. *Programs*—deciding what programs will reach your potential audience and help fulfill God's purposes;
5. *Process*—displaying your programs so you can help students move toward spiritual maturity;
6. *Planned values*—defining what values will strengthen your ministry and enhance your purposes;
7. *Parents*—teaming up with the family for a stronger youth ministry and church;
8. *Participating leaders*—finding volunteers and developing them into ministers who fulfill the purposes;
9. *Perseverance*—learning how to survive the overwhelming responsibilities, discipline problems, and the adventure of change.[7]

Fields begins by noting his own pilgrimage from the typical youth minister who frantically tries to please people, provide programs, and create the "hype." His honest confession—how he learned that his walk with God was paramount—demonstrates the need of the hour in youth ministry. What did he learn? "No youth ministry idea or program can compete with God's power working in and through you as he gives you a passion for students and you give him a pure heart."[8] Enough of youth ministry focuses on programs and techniques; we need passion and truth. Fields' book will help you build a solid ministry to youth, and raise the bar in the areas I've noted above and throughout this book.

A similar passion is seen in *The Seven Checkpoints* by Stanley and Hall, where content, they argue, should drive context:

It is one thing to put together a summer camp. It is quite another thing to create the optimal five-day environment for teenagers to rethink their whole approach to friendship. . . .

When content is the focus, the context becomes vitally important. This approach to youth ministry will motivate you and your leadership to raise the bar programmatically.[9]

Stanley and Hall offer the following seven checkpoints to build a youth ministry:

1. *Authentic faith*—God can be trusted;
2. *Spiritual disciplines*—devotional life;
3. *Moral boundaries*—personal purity;
4. *Healthy friendships*—choosing friends;
5. *Wise choices*—decision making;
6. *Ultimate authority*—submission to God's authority;
7. *Others first*—humility and service.[10]

Fields' model, and that of Stanley and Hall, address significantly the important issues of the Christian life. But churches can raise the bar yet higher in the vital areas of theological truth and biblical knowledge, and the practical area of personal evangelism. Still, both of the above models can help to serve as a way to evaluate your youth ministry.

Jay Strack, longtime youth evangelist, has devoted much of his time in recent years to his Student Leadership University to equip the cream of the crop of Christian students. "The best young people we have may be straight and clean . . . which we thank God for," Strack says in the Student Life University Introductory Video. "But for the most part [they] are not making an impact on society." Strack believes this is less because of youth themselves and more because of the low standards we've set for them. As one young lady in the video observed, "We don't teach youth to dream, we teach them to settle." Student Leadership University—having venues in Orlando, Florida; Washington, D.C.; and two European cities—takes Christian students to a higher level, training them in four stages. (You can visit Student Leadership University at www.studentleadership.net.)

Youth ministry should, then, be a mirror of the church. Purpose derived from Scripture should guide all we do. This includes special events like camps. If we pay a lot for children to go to basketball camp, we expect them to come back with more skill. The same or more should be expected from church camp! How much more should we expect from youth ministry?

Dr. Reid,

I have recently moved to the Midwest after going through a tough time in my life. I was one of those discontented youth pastors you talked about in the article "Raising the Bar." Like most of the youth pastors I went to seminary with, I was ready to get out of youth ministry and do something "deeper." Then God did something wonderful in my heart over the last three years. I am the new Youth and Families pastor at my church and I am passionate about doing "youth ministry" again! I recently read some of Mark DeVries' material and also Dr. Black's book "The Myth of Adolescence." I am working to prepare myself to be a better youth worker over the long haul of my life. So I started reading Augustine, Calvin, Bunyan, Black, Devries, and above all, The Bible! Imagine that! I am thanking God for second chances!

I would be grateful for any recommendations, advice, etc. you could give to a thirty-two-year old youth pastor who is starting over.

Joy,
Cliff

This e-mail represents so many youth pastors who are sick and tired of working themselves to death while seeing little spiritual truth taking hold in their students. A renewed focus is the need of the hour. Frank Voight wrote a classic story called "The Lifesaving Station." This simple parable illustrates how those of us in ministry must focus on reaching people who live on the brink of eternity in hell:

On a dangerous seacoast where shipwrecks often occur was a crude, little lifesaving station. The building was just a hut, and there was only one boat. The few devoted members kept a constant watch over the sea. With no thought for themselves, they went out, day or night, searching tirelessly for the lost. So many lives were saved by the wonderful little station that it became famous.

Some of those who were saved, and various others in the surrounding area, wanted to become associated with the station and gave of their time, money, and effort for the support of its work. New boats were bought, and new crews were trained.

Some of the new members of the lifesaving station were unhappy because the building was crude and poorly equipped. They felt that a more comfortable place should be provided as the first refuge of those saved from the sea. So they replaced the emergency cots with beds and put better furniture in an enlarged building.

Now the lifesaving station became a popular gathering place for its members, and they redecorated it beautifully and furnished it exquisitely because they used it as a club. Fewer members were now interested in going to sea on lifesaving missions so they hired crews to do this work. The lifesaving motif still prevailed in the club decoration, however.

About this time, a large ship was wrecked off the coast, and the hired crew brought in boatloads of cold, wet, and half-drowned people. They were dirty and sick; some had black skin, and some had yellow skin. The beautiful club was considerably messed up. So the property committee immediately had a shower house built outside the club where victims of shipwrecks could be cleaned up before coming inside.

At the next meeting, a split took place in the club membership. Most of the members wanted to stop the lifesaving activities as they were unpleasant and a hindrance to the normal life of the club. Some members insisted on lifesaving as their primary purpose and pointed out that they still were called a lifesaving station. They finally were voted down, however, and told that if they wanted to save the lives of various kinds of people who were shipwrecked in those waters, they could begin their own lifesaving station down the coast. They did.

As the years went by, the new station experienced the same changes that had occurred in the old. It evolved into a club, and yet another lifesaving station was founded. History continued to repeat itself; and if you visit that coast today, you will find a number of exclusive clubs along that shore. Shipwrecks are still frequent in those waters. But most people drown.[11]

It is tragic when a person lives a life with no purpose. The most tragic thing, however, is to be given a mission, a purpose, a reason to live, and then to lose sight of it. If you are a Christian who leads youth, regardless of your position, you are called to bring people to Jesus and to push those who meet Him into a radical walk with the Lord. It's time to get in the boat, and go save some drowning people.

Chapter Thirteen

Rites of Passage

For I know the thoughts that I think toward you, says the
LORD, thoughts of peace and not of evil, to give you a fu-
ture and a hope.

—Jeremiah 29:11

Four hundred men met at 5:30—on a Monday *morning!* John Avant, one of my best friends, fellow dad, and pastor of New Hope Baptist Church near Atlanta, told me about the meeting. They were a group of men hungry to be better dads, and early morning was the only time that seemed to work for them. He asked the men, "How many of you had dads who took time to teach you what it means to be a man?" Out of four hundred men, only three raised their hands.

I worked as a carpenter with some very lost people as I finished college and prepared for seminary. The foreman took his son to see a prostitute on his sixteenth birthday. He thought that was a great way to help his son become a man. While that detestable act demonstrates criminal neglect and supreme foolishness, can we as believers be so critical? How many of us fail to be intentional in helping our children grow up to be men and women of God? Michelle and I do a lot with students and are very active at church. But we know that nothing in our lives matters more than helping Josh and Hannah become adults who are passionate followers of Jesus.

As I began to present my ideas for raising the bar in lectures at scholarly meetings and when training youth ministers, I encountered some who have also given much thought to the matter of helping kids be godly. For them the most consistent question they raised was about rites of passage.

I am indebted to my colleague David Alan Black's book *The Myth of*

Adolescence and Robert Lewis's *Raising a Modern-Day Knight* as key sources to helping me think through three matters with my own son. Lewis says fathers are failing their sons at three points:

1. ***Defining Manhood:*** "Telling a boy to 'be a man' without defining manhood is like saying, 'be a success.' It sounds good. But, practically, it takes you nowhere."
2. ***Directional Process:*** "What [a son] needs is a specific language and training that takes him to the place where, like the apostle Paul, he can say, 'When I became a man, I did away with childish things.'"
3. ***Ceremony:*** "How many dads today think of formally commemorating their sons' progress or passage to manhood? Very few."[1]

Lewis notes the case of Jeffrey Dahmer. Dahmer, who performed the gruesome killings of seventeen people, was convicted in 1992 and was killed by an inmate two years later. He was raised by his mother and father. Dahmer's story is not, then, the tale of a broken home. It's the story of a dad who was around geographically, but not *there* emotionally.

Dylan Klebold and Eric Harris—the gunmen at Columbine—lived with their parents. So troubled youth cannot be blamed simply on broken homes. My wife was raised in a single-parent home, but she grew up to be a godly, wonderful wife and mother. So while the breakdown of the family is a huge factor in youth problems, other causes are far more complex. Raising well-adjusted and motivated youth derives enormous benefit from a solid marriage, but it must include more.

Theories of child raising abound, each trailed by controversy over its validity. But there's one fact that all parents agree upon. Life changes when you have kids. Theories about child-rearing move instantly from the hypothetical to the real. It's one thing to give advice to others based on your theory of this or that; it's altogether another thing to apply those theories to your own children.

So when my son approached the youth years, I suddenly found myself caring little for some expert's theory on how to raise a teen. I cared only about two things: first, what does God say about raising my son; second, how can I take what He says and live it out before my children?

By the grace of God I found some godly help. A fellow dad, a layman with children several years older than mine (and far ahead of their peers spiritually), modeled how to be a father. Other books and friends, all of which will be noted in the following pages, helped as well.

From these sources, I derived the importance of rites of passage—ceremonies that mark critical steps in a young person's life. The Bible teaches baptism as a significant rite in the life of a believer. Following conversion, baptism serves as a significant ceremony, publicly demonstrating the believer's identification with Christ. Marriage is another beautiful ceremony that marks both an achievement and a life-changing event. In my church, we observe the dedication of a child, which actually is the dedication of the *parents,* celebrated in a meaningful ceremony. But what then for that child?

We've replaced ceremonies with banquets, and we've trivialized important steps in the lives of young adults. Now we no longer teach or recognize such steps. It's time for a rebirth of rites of passage. But these will be significant only if they serve to mark genuine turning points in the lives of those participating in such ceremonies.

Our culture does have rites of passage: moving from middle school to high school, obtaining a driver's license, graduating from high school. These are still officially recognized but are the property of culture, not the church. Other rites are more unofficial, such as losing one's virginity or getting drunk the first time.

So when Josh turned twelve, I marked it by taking him on a mission trip to Chicago. We talked about a lot of things, and we also went to a Cubs game at Wrigley. The bottom line is this: I told Josh he was now a young man, not a little boy. His mother and I expected him to behave like a young man, that we'd allow Josh as much freedom as he could handle, based on how much responsibility he could bear. We didn't try to make him an instant adult, but we did begin allowing him to make adult decisions as he could manage them.

The result has been incredible. By age twelve he was already playing congas in the adult praise band at our church. By thirteen and a half he had led several people to Christ, including adults far his senior. He's shown a strong capacity for leadership, while certainly reminding us almost daily that he's not perfect.

Although I'm not convinced that the evangelical church will come to a consensus on what rites of passage to observe or how, I pray that we'll all come to a conviction about the importance of raising up a generation of godly young men and women. To that end, here are some possible transitions/rites.

Age twelve. David Black refers to this age as the Age Twelve Transition, one of the most vital turning points of life. At age twelve, Jesus was in the temple, teaching about His heavenly Father. He and other Jewish youth went through a Bar Mitzvah ceremony. Even to the present day, this ceremony is seen as "a period when young people are obligated to control their own desires, accept responsibility for mature religious actions, and assume adult community responsibilities."[2] In the twentieth century, the Bat Miztvah was developed for young ladies.

For centuries, cultures around the world have recognized a time of turning toward adulthood at about this age:

- Sitting Bull, the mighty chief, spent days alone in the wilderness at this age;
- Masai tribesmen have a similar ceremony, as do young men in Nigeria and other African cultures;
- Amish boys in some areas are taught to run the entire farm around age twelve.

Black in *Myth of Adolescence* offers excellent advice on and examples of how to hold a ceremony. This includes both a public ceremony and a private letter from a parent to a child.

> Robert Lewis set four times to mark rites of passage: puberty, high school graduation, college graduation, and marriage. I personally like to emphasize the age of sixteen and the driver's license as another.

Increasing numbers of evangelical parents are taking their children through a service similar to this when their child turns twelve. Imagine the youth pastor or another significant adult in your church taking the parents and the student to a meal, where he explains the purpose of the vital years to come and the church's role—to help their child to adulthood. This would be not only a good starting point for raising the bar, but could be a means of witness to unchurched parents. Parents actively involved in your church could be shown how to observe a Christian Bar Mitzvah or similar ceremony.

While the age of twelve rite is the major turning point, other ceremonies like the following could help to guide a youth into adulthood.

Age fourteen or eighth grade. A True Love Waits or similar commitment to purity is optional, but given the obsession with sexuality in our culture, a time of serious teaching and a time of public consecration to moral purity has been shown to be quite effective.

Age sixteen. Paralleling the major step of responsibility of a driver's license, a ceremony or perhaps a banquet when a youth turns sixteen is an excellent way to convey to a person what it means to be a man or woman of God. A group of men, highly respected as Christians, taking time individually to explain to a young man turning sixteen what it means to be a godly man could have a lifelong impact. The same could be said for a young lady. In the case of my son, I plan to have each guest bring a printed copy of his comments for me to put into a special binder for Josh to keep his whole life.

Age sixteen is already a critical transition in American culture. A young person getting his or her driver's license has huge implications for youth ministry. So many youth become less involved in church at the time they get their car and have more control over their time. Lower involvement can be laid partly to parents, as an alarming number of church youth are not only allowed but encouraged to work secular jobs on Sundays. And we wonder why they drop out of church when they are on their own. They learn it from their churchgoing parents!

Youth ministries can provide valuable assistance to families by helping parents prepare their children for the vital step of responsibility of driving. Rather than bemoaning the decline of church attendance by older youth who drive, churches can provide more challenging ministries using the growing maturity and responsibility of students. As young people move from the "do it because I tell you" relationship with their parents, to an increasing ability and need to make responsible decisions on their own, churches can help students step up spiritually even as they grow up socially.

Age eighteen or high school graduation—missions. While your children are still young, set a standard for them to give a summer, semester, or year following high school to the mission field. Begin challenging youth to prepare for spending the first year of their lives after high school in missions somewhere around the world. What a way to unleash an army to the world!

The Mormons can be our teachers in this area, because for Mormons, the highlight of their lives is their mission, undertaken while young. In fact, if a religious body were a football team, the Mormons would put their youth on the first string. I'm afraid that most of our churches wouldn't let their youth on the practice squad. There has been no greater time, though, in recent history to challenge students to consider God's call to missions or other ministry callings. If we issued that challenge, we could see another Student Volunteer Movement in the next decade. God is able, are we hopeful?

Richard and Joan Ostling demonstrate how the Mormon mission provides a rite of passage that generally keeps followers in the LDS movement their entire lives:

> The universal lay priesthood, including the emphasis on two-year missionary assignments, is no doubt a major reason why LDS children remain loyal and involved through adolescence and young adulthood. Everybody from age twelve is incorporated into the system with special status. . . . As a deacon, he distributes the sacraments, collects past offerings, cares for the buildings and grounds, and helps otherwise. . . . Between the ages of fourteen and sixteen he becomes a teacher. . . . Finally, he becomes a priest between the ages of sixteen and eighteen. He can teach and exhort during home teaching sessions, baptize, administer the sacrament, and ordain teachers and deacons to the priesthood.[3]

Marriage. Nothing, other than conversion, matters more than marriage. This is the only rite of passage today still deemed worthy by most to be consistently recognized as a ceremony. But if earlier rites were observed, might not adults be more prepared for this vital covenant?

Along the way, give youth increasing types of chores and responsibilities around the house. Teach them to be responsible with their finances. (Tithing started early makes a difference!) Let them lead in church to the level they can. I'm thankful that our church utilizes all ages in drama, praise band, and other areas of leadership. This could be an area your church needs to examine.

A Word to Fathers

At a youth camp in 2002 I gave the "guy" talk to the males. Before delving into the sex talk, I took about five minutes and told them a few things to do for the young ladies: opening doors for them, giving up their seat in a crowded room, and letting them go first in line. I told them to treat ladies with respect. These teenagers looked at me as if I were speaking in a foreign language. "How many of you have never heard this before?" I asked. Many, many hands went up.

The days following I was deluged by teenaged young ladies and female counselors thanking me, because the guys began practicing what they heard me preach. Weeks later I continued to receive e-mails testifying to a change in the behavior of young men. These young men were ready and willing to be more gentlemanly, but no one had told them how.

Young men learn to be rude. They learn to be gross. They learn to speak coarsely to ladies. And the feminist agenda over the past few years has caused too many dads to fail when it comes to teaching their sons how to treat the opposite sex with honor and respect. It seems that the radical feminist movement in America has not only robbed women of their femininity, it's robbed men of their masculinity. But I refuse to bow to the policies of the politically correct. It is a sad day when the word *gentlemen* is only seen on bathroom doors or on signs advertising adult strip clubs.

As illustrated at the beginning of this chapter, dads teaching their sons how to be men has lost priority. Dads today weren't taught it themselves, so they don't know where to start. (And are moms teaching their daughters what it means to be not only a woman, but a *lady?* Is not the problem of teenaged ladies dressing immodestly an issue their mothers should address?)

How is a dad to teach a son to be a man? Lewis gives helpful counsel:

1. *A real man rejects passivity.* I spoke to a men's retreat in Denver, Colorado. In a demonstration of brokenness, a leader in the church confessed, "My son has been a problem lately, becoming more rebellious. How have I dealt with this? I simply started working longer hours." This man's candid confession demonstrates our culture's view of Dad as a provider above all else. But this dad realized he was simply being passive, hiding at work, hoping the problem would go away.

2. *A real man accepts responsibility.* Dads, you are responsible for your children's spiritual nurture. Yet so many dads relinquish this to moms or to the church. It is biblically inconsistent and personally irresponsible for a father to be known as a reliable worker at the office, a dependable volunteer at church, yet be uninvolved in the spiritual, emotional, and relational upbringing of his children.

3. *A real man leads courageously.* The quota for Christian wimps has been met. Dads, good for you if you provide for your family, but even lost dads do that. Do your children see you stand courageously for Jesus?

4. *A real man expects the greater reward.* I have an incredible job. I teach the greatest students on earth, get to preach in some of the finest churches in America, and have written many books. But all that pales in comparison to my family. I've turned down some incredible opportunities—leading a major prayer summit by Promise Keepers; speaking to the largest crowd in my life in Asia. Other opportunities have come and gone. Yet I refused to accept them. Why? Because I already made a commitment to my family. I believe God rewards faithfulness more than opportunism. Don't misunderstand; at times I've missed family events or a ball game for the Lord. I don't believe the family should be an idol. But after God Himself, my family is my #2 priority. My ministry is #3.[4]

Men, your children need you to be godly. The daughters of men who are not godly models and who do not show fatherly affection grow into insecure young women who often become sexually active at a young age. The sons of men who do not teach their boys how to be men cannot deal well with anger or are confused about their sexuality.

Richard Baxter, the great Puritan pastor of centuries past, said the only way we will see true reformation is to see it first in the home. Increasingly, parents are discovering the truth of Baxter's remark. Organizations like the Council on Biblical Manhood and Womanhood seek to share the biblical way to family life in the face of feminism and other assaults on the home.

I've spoken a lot about my relationship with Josh, my firstborn. I could fill a book this size with my parental failures, unanswered questions, and missed opportunities. But one thing I've learned: our children care more about our passion for them and for God than how perfect we are in living before them.

In his eighth-grade class Josh and his peers wrote an essay about the person they most admire. My son's paper proves that what I'm writing is more than theory.

The Person I Most Admire

My dad is the one person who has had the biggest impact on my life. He works as the professor of evangelism at Southeastern Baptist Theological Seminary in Wake Forest, North Carolina. Of course, he is very active in church because he preaches all the time.

The first reason I admire my dad is because he is a godly man. He preaches in around twenty to twenty-five states per year, but he doesn't make a big deal about it. He also writes books that are challenging to teenagers. Sometimes I don't understand why he does all this stuff for God, but I'm glad he does.

The next, and probably most special reason, is that he loves my family and me. He shows his love to us mainly by the way he talks about us in public. Every now and then he will do something spontaneous (like buying my mom a dog). He also takes my sister and me on trips that he doesn't need to spend his extra money on. These are the reasons I love him and the rest of my family so much.

The third, and my favorite reason, is he is just a fun guy to be around. During my basketball games, he is the loudest freak in the bleachers! He loves to cut up and tell funny, corny jokes. He can also be annoying sometimes. That is my favorite thing because sometimes I can be annoying, too.

You can see why I admire my dad. He is a godly man, he loves me and my family, and he is just fun to be around. I know he and I will always be not only father and son, but also best friends. I am very thankful to have such a special dad.

All the books, preaching in great churches, the wonderful friendships I've made with some of the most godly people on earth—all pale in comparison to knowing that God has given me such a great relationship with Josh. It's a lot of work but, in his own words, Josh has told me that the work has been well worth it.

Conclusion

A Radical Challenge

To sum up, this is what youth ministers must do:

1. Stop treating youth like children who are finishing childhood, and start treating them like young adults moving into adulthood. The myth of adolescence is just that—a myth;
2. Reduce the segregation of youth from the life of the church;
3. Raise the bar in what we teach in terms of both biblical orthodoxy *and* orthopraxy. *Belief,* not only behavior, must be changed;
4. Do more to strengthen the family. A feature in our culture was not, however, an issue until recent days: the large divorce rate and the unprecedented numbers of youth coming to churches without parents;
5. Make a distinction between explicit biblical teaching and valid principles we can apply to this culture;
6. Prepare this new generation to take on the whole world.

In 1995 I was a professor at Houston Baptist University in Texas. During that time, God was doing remarkable things in some local churches and on some college campuses. A spirit of revival touched many, and was recorded in books, on radio, and via e-mail. In February of that year I spoke at a church near Houston, where the hand of God moved powerfully. The service continued for hours, and I never even preached my prepared sermon! Instead, I had asked students from Brownwood, Texas, and Howard Payne University to share a testimony of what God had done on their campus and at their church, Coggin Avenue Baptist.

That night, a fifteen-year-old girl stood and, weeping, shared with the church that she had just learned she was pregnant. This broken young lady confessed her sin, and people in the church ministered to her. She decided to keep the baby rather than opting for abortion, and it was my understanding that she would give up the baby for adoption. I later told her story briefly in a book about the movement.

Do you ever wonder if your ministry really matters long term? Since my ministry in churches is of an itinerant nature, I sometimes wonder what happens to those whom I see God touch. In the case above, I never met with the young lady. I never knew her name. I wrote three paragraphs about her and have told her story in many places.

Recently, eight years later, I went to work, turned on my computer, and checked my e-mail. This is what I read:

Dr. Reid,

I am not sure if you remember me, but I was the fifteen-year-old pregnant girl. I wanted to let you know that I recently sought out a copy of the book and began to read it for the first time in many years, and the passage about me brought me to tears. I wanted to thank you for putting my story in there. . . . I was glad to read something done entirely by a stranger and get an outside perspective of that situation after [finding] healing. I would love it if that passage in some, even small, way helped another person, but just for myself it was nice to remember some of the details that I had forgotten.

I also wanted to give you an update on me. I recently graduated [from college] and am married to the most wonderful man I have ever known. I am planning on going to medical school and becoming a pediatrician.

I placed my two-day-old son for adoption. . . . He is a wonderful, almost eight-year-old, stubborn boy. His parents are wonderful and I am truly blessed to be allowed the chance to know him as he grows. He and his younger brother were ring bearers at my wedding. I could not imagine what my life would have been like without him.

Marium

I wept like a baby when I read the e-mail. Readers, whatever you do in the lives of young people, it matters. Find some youth. Raise the bar. Set the standard high. And love them. A generation could be different as a result.

Endnotes

Introduction

1. Taken from Lynn Vincent, "Gunpoint Evangelist," *World*, 9 October 1999, 16–19.
2. Dan Crawford, *Night of Tragedy, Dawning of Light* (Wheaton, Ill.: Harold Shaw, 2000), 69.

Chapter 1: Meet the Millennials

1. Misty Bernall, *She Said Yes* (Farmington, Pa.: Plough, 1999), ix.
2. George Barna, *Real Teens: A Contemporary Snapshot of Youth Culture* (Ventura, Calif.: Regal, 2001), 13.
3. Neil Howe and William Strauss, *Millennials Rising: The Next Great Generation* (New York: Vintage, 2000).
4. Ibid., 3.
5. Ibid., 4.
6. See ibid., 7ff.
7. Barna, *Real Teens*, 46.
8. From Howe and Strauss, *Millennials Rising*, 4.
9. Barna, *Real Teens*, 68.
10. Mike Males, "The Culture War Against Kids," AlterNet, 22 May 2001: http://alternet.org/story.html?StoryID=10904. Accessed 12 March 2002.

11. Chris Lehmann, "Teen-Demon Tracts: Why baby-boomer parents fear their children," February 2002: http://www.magportal.com/cgi-bin/rdir. cgi?w=87689. Accessed 12 March 2002.

12. Ibid.

13. Howe and Strauss, *Millennials Rising,* 218.

14. Katharine Mieszkowski, "Thank God for the Internet: 'Next' author Michael Lewis says that the Net makes lawyers look foolish and Wall Street analysts irrelevant," 18 July 2001: http://adfarm.mediaplex.com/ad/fm/ 1222-5050-1101-0?mpt=2002.03.14.00.15.48. Accessed 12 February 2002.

15. Barna, *Real Teens,* 83.

16. Ibid, 86.

17. The ratio of youth to the total population will still be less than the Boomer years of the 1970s because of abortion.

18. Howe and Strauss, *Millennials Rising,* 10.

19. Jim Collins, *Good to Great* (New York: Harper Business, 2001), 1.

Chapter 2: Time to Climatize

1. Richard Ross and Len Taylor, *Leading an Evangelistic Youth Ministry* (Nashville: Lifeway, 1999), 8.

2. Jonathan Edwards, "Some Thoughts Concerning the Present Revival of Religion in New England, and the Way in Which It Ought to Be Acknowledged and Promoted, Humbly Offered to the Public, in a Treatise on That Subject," in *The Works of Jonathan Edwards,* 2 vols., ed. Sereno E. Dwight (1834; reprint, London: Banner of Truth Trust, nd.), 1:423.

3. Greg Stier, *Outbreak: Creating a Contagious Youth Ministry Through Viral Evangelism* (Chicago: Moody, 2002), 17.

4. Louie Giglio, foreword to *The Seven Checkpoints,* by Andy Stanley and Stuart Hall (West Monroe, La.: Howard, 2001), x.

5. Mark DeVries, "What Is Youth Ministry's Relationship to the Family?" in *Reaching a Generation for Christ,* ed. Richard R. Dunn and Mark H. Centers III (Chicago: Moody, 1997), 484–85.

6. George Barna, *Real Teens: A Contemporary Snapshot of Youth Culture* (Ventura, Calif.: Regal, 2001), 113.

7. Ibid.

8. Ibid., 112.

9. Ibid., 132.

10. John Detonni, "Putting Youth Ministry into Perspective," in *Reaching a Generation for Christ,* 27–28.

11. To get a copy of the twenty-eight-day prayer guide, go to www.alvinreid.com/ articles.

Chapter 3: The Potency of Expectancy

1. John Cloud, "Just a Routine School Shooting," *Time,* 31 May 1999, 58.

2. Barry St. Clair, foreword to *Outbreak: Creating a Contagious Youth Ministry Through Viral Evangelism,* by Greg Stier (Chicago: Moody, 2002), 10.

3. George Barna, *Real Teens: A Contemporary Snapshot of Youth Culture* (Ventura, Calif.: Regal, 2001), 15–16.

4. Greg Stier, *Outbreak: Creating Contagious Youth Ministry Through Viral Evangelism* (Chicago: Moody, 2002), 21.

5. Marva Dawn, *Reaching Out Without Dumbing Down* (Grand Rapids: Zondervan, 1995), 17.

6. Barna, *Real Teens,* 80.

7. Michael Lewis, *Next: The Future Just Happened* (New York: Norton, 2002); cited in Katharine Mieszkowski, "Thank God for the Internet: 'Next' author Michael Lewis says that the Net makes lawyers look foolish and Wall Street analysts irrelevant," 18 July 2001: http://adfarm.mediaplex.com/ad/fm/ 1222-5050-1101-0?mpt=2002.03.14.00.15.48. Accessed 12 February 2002.

8. Stier, *Outbreak,* 60.

9. Ibid., 61.

Chapter 4: Truth or Consequences

1. See, for example, James Davidson Hunter, *Evangelicalism: The Coming Generation* (Chicago: University of Chicago Press, 1988).

2. David Alan Black, *The Myth of Adolescence* (Yorba Linda, Calif.: Davidson, 1998), 19.

3. Ibid., 6ff.

4. Ibid., 22.

5. Lance Morrow, "The Boys and the Bees: The Shootings Are One More Argument for Abolishing Adolescence," *Time,* 31 May 1999, 110.

6. Ibid.

7. Ibid.

8. David Bakan, "Adolescence in America: From Idea to Social Fact," *Daedalus* 100 (1971): 979–95; cited in Black, *Myth of Adolescence*, 15.

9. Black, *Myth of Adolescence*, 17.

Chapter 5: Entertaining Children or Assembling an Army

1. I first began to think through the role of students in the history of the church in "The Zeal of Youth: The Role of Students in the History of Awakenings," in *Evangelism for a Changing World*, eds. Timothy Beougher and Alvin L. Reid (Wheaton, Ill.: Harold Shaw, 1995).

2. Philip Spener, *Pia Desiteria* (1675); Fortress continues to publish the book, illustrating its status as a classic in Christian spirituality.

3. Earle E. Cairns, *An Endless Line of Splendor: Revivals and Their Leaders from the Great Awakening to the Present* (Wheaton, Ill.: Tyndale House, 1986), 34.

4. See David Howard, "Student Power in World Missions," in *Perspectives on the World Christian Movement*, ed. Ralph Winter (Pasadena: William Carey, 1981), 211–14.

5. For more about the Great Awakenings, see Malcolm McDow and Alvin L. Reid, *Firefall: How God Shaped History Through Revivals* (Enumclaw, Wash.: Pleasant Word, 2002). For information on youth in the history of revival, see Alvin L. Reid, *Light the Fire: Raising Up a Generation to Live Radically for Jesus* (Enumclaw, Wash: Winepress, 2000).

6. Jonathan Edwards, "A Faithful Narrative of the Surprising Work of God, in the Conversion of Many Hundred Souls, in Northampton, and the Neighbouring Towns and Villages of New Hampshire, in New England; in a Letter to the Rev. Dr. Colman, of Boston," in *The Works of Jonathan Edwards*, 2 vols., ed. Sereno E. Dwight (1834; reprint, London: Banner of Truth Trust, n.d) 1:347.

7. Ibid.

8. See W. W. Sweet, *The Story of Religion in America* (New York: Harper and Brothers, 1930), 140.

9. George Whitefield, *The Journals of George Whitefield* (reprint, Edinburgh: Banner of Truth Trust, 1960), 354.

10. Earle Cairns, *Endless Line of Splendor* (Wheaton, Ill.: Tyndale House, 1982), 42.

11. Quoted from Hill's biography in Arthur Dicken Thomas Jr., "Reasonable

Revivalism: Presbyterian Evangelization of Educated Virginians, 1787–1837," *Journal of Presbyterian History* 61 (fall 1983): 322.

12. Ibid., 322ff.

13. See Chauncy A. Goodrich, "Narrative of Revivals of Religion in Yale College," *American Quarterly Register* 10 (February 1838): 295–96.

14. Ibid.

15. See Gardiner Spring, *Memoir of Samuel John Mills* (Boston: Perkins and Marvin, 1829) and Thomas Richards, *Samuel J. Mills: Missionary Pathfinder, Pioneer, and Promoter* (Boston: Pilgrim, 1906).

16. See Bennett Tyler, ed., *New England Revivals, as They Existed at the Close of the Eighteenth Century, and the Beginning of the Nineteenth Centuries* (reprint, Wheaton, Ill.: Richard Owen Roberts, 1980); J. Edwin Orr, *Campus Aflame* (reprint, Wheaton, Ill.: International Awakening, 1992); and John Avant, Malcolm McDow, and Alvin L. Reid, *Revival: An Account of the Current Revival in Brownwood, Fort Worth, Wheaton and Beyond* (Nashville: Broadman and Holman, 1995).

17. J. Edwin Orr, *Fervent Prayer* (Chicago: Moody, 1974), 11–12.

18. John Pollock, *Moody* (Chicago: Moody, 1983), 34.

19. Ibid.

Chapter 6: The Jesus Movement

1. Duane Pederson, *Jesus People* (Ventura, Calif.: Regal, 1971), 34–35.

2. "Street Christians: Jesus as the Ultimate Trip," *Time,* 3 August 1970, 31.

3. Walker L. Knight, "Faddists or Disciples?" in *Jesus People Come Alive,* comp. Walker L. Knight (Wheaton, Ill.: Tyndale House, 1971), 103.

4. Pederson, *Jesus People,* 36, 103.

5. Erling Jorstad, *That New-Time Religion* (Minneapolis: Augsburg, 1972), 55.

6. Larry R. Jerden, "Surf and Soul," *Baptist Standard,* 13 August 1969, 12–13; Michael McFadden, *The Jesus Revolution* (New York: Harper and Row, 1972), 14; and Edward E. Plowman, *The Jesus Movement in America* (Elgin, Ill.: David C. Cook, 1971), 58.

7. Edward E. Plowman, *The Jesus People* (Elgin, Ill.: David C. Cook, 1971), 24.

8. McFadden, *Jesus Revolution,* 11.

9. Toby Druin, "Echoes of the Movement," *Home Missions,* June–July 1971, 46.

10. Plowman, *Jesus Movement in America*, 110–11; and "9,000 Attend Chicago Rally," *Indiana Baptist*, 29 March 1971, 8. Duane Pederson was the speaker the next month. "'Jesus Festival' Presents Him," *Arkansas Baptist Newsmagazine*, 2 November 1972, 9.

11. See Plowman, *Jesus Movement in America*, 55; "1,000 Baptized in California Ocean," *Indiana Baptist*, 23 June 1971, 6; and Jess C. Moody, audio interview on tape recording, 13 August 1990, Indianapolis (copy in hand of author).

12. "The Jesus People," 97.

13. For a concise account of the Asbury Revival, see Robert E. Coleman, ed., *One Divine Moment* (Old Tappan, N.J.: Revell, 1970).

14. See Malcolm McDow and Alvin L. Reid, *Firefall: How God Shaped History Through Revivals* (Enumclaw, Wash.: Pleasant Word, 2002), for many examples of church growth coming from awakenings.

15. Walker A. Knight, "Prelude to a Spiritual Awakening," *Missions USA*, March–April 1982, 21.

16. "Memories of the Jesus Movement," 18-20. For an analysis of the ministry of Horizon see Towns, *Ten of Today's Most Innovative Churches*, (Ventura, Calif.: Regal, 1990), 150-62.

17. *National and International Religion Report.* 23 September 1991, 8.

18. Hadaway, DuBose, and Wright, 114-29.

19. Bill Hybels, "Full Circle," *Willow Creek Magazine Special Anniversary Issue*, vol. 2, November–December 1990,10. For a complete and fascinating look at Willow Creek see Lynne and Bill Hybels, *Rediscovering Church* (Grand Rapids: Zondervan, 1995).

20. "Into the Stratosphere," *Willow Creek Magazine Special Anniversary Issue*, vol. 2, November–December 1990, 20.

21. Knight, "The Jesus Movement Revisited," 4.

22. For example, see the weakening of conviction expressed in such views as inclusivism in such writers as John Sanders, Clark Pinnock, and Stanley Grenz.

23. "Will the Church Join or Run?" *Baptist Standard*, 30 June 1971, 4.

24. The best historical discussion on this subject is Jonathan Edwards' classic *Distinguishing Marks* in *The Complete Works of Jonathan Edwards*, ed. Sereno E. Dwight (reprint, Edinburgh: The Banner of Truth Trust: 1986).

Chapter 7: Life Is Short. Pray Hard

1. Lani Hinkle, *Pray!* September–October 1998, 22.
2. Art Toalston, "'We Still Pray' Aims to Go National with Rallies, Prayer at Football Games," *Baptist Press Release,* 22 August 2000.
3. Ibid. "An Awesome Way to Pray" resources are available from Lifeway Christian Resources. For more information or to order, call 800-458-2772.
4. Mike Higgs, "Lead Us, Join Us, or Get Out of the Way!" *Pray!* September–October 1998, 8.
5. Ibid., 19.
6. John Avant, Malcolm McDow, and Alvin Reid, *Revival!* (Nashville: Broadman and Holman, 1996), 47.
7. I am indebted to my friend Dough Murton who has helped me think through this idea.
8. S. D. Gordon in Dutch Sheets, *Intercessory Prayer.* (Ventura, Calif.: Regal, 1996), 23.
9. These are adapted from my book *Introduction to Evangelism* (Nashville: Broadman and Holman, 1998), 144–45.
10. George Barna, *Real Teens: A Contemporary Snapshot of Youth Culture* (Ventura, Calif.: Regal, 2001), 35–37.
11. Greg Stier, *Outbreak: Creating a Contagious Youth Ministry Through Viral Evangelism* (Chicago: Moody, 2002), 107.
12. Ibid., 108.

Chapter 8: Teaching the Youth Well

1. Richard Dunn, "Putting Youth Ministry into Perspective," in *Reaching a Generation for Christ,* ed. Richard R. Dunn and Mark H. Centers III (Chicago: Moody, 1997), 31–32.
2. Greg Stier, *Outbreak: Creating a Contagious Youth Ministry Through Viral Evangelism* (Chicago: Moody, 2002), 19.
3. George Barna, *Real Teens: A Contemporary Snapshot of Youth Culture* (Ventura, Calif.: Regal, 2001), 132.
4. Ibid., 135.
5. Barna in Jon Walker, "Youngest Generation Comfortable with Contradictions," http://www.pastors.com/article.asp?ArtID=3471. Accessed 4 February 2001.

6. See Alvin L. Reid, *Radically Unchurched: Who They Are and How to Reach Them* (Grand Rapids: Kregel, 2002).
7. InQuest Ministries (www.inquest.org) provides some of the best materials I have found.
8. Neil Howe and William Strauss, *Millennials Rising: The Next Great Generation* (New York: Vintage, 2000), 7.
9. Barna, *Real Teens,* 135–36.
10. Ibid., 155–56.
11. For information on Go Tell Camps, go to www.rickgageministries.com.
12. Barna, *Real Teens,* 94.
13. Andy Stanley and Stuart Hall, *The Seven Checkpoints* (West Monroe, La.: Howard, 2001), 4.
14. Josh McDowell, *The Disconnected Generation* (Nashville: Word, 2000).
15. "Three Cries of the Post-Modern Student," www.inquest.org/pmstudent.htm. Accessed 30 December 2003.
16. "How Would Jesus Reach the Post-Modern Student?" www.inquest.org/creating.htm. Accessed 30 December 2003.

Chapter 9: Get Real

1. George Barna, *Real Teens: A Contemporary Snapshot of Youth Culture* (Ventura, Calif.: Regal, 2001), 16.
2. Charles Haddon Spurgeon, *Lectures to My Students* (Lynchburg, Va.: Old-Time Gospel Hour, 1875), 36.
3. Check out Frontliners at www.frontliners.org.
4. Richard Ross and Len Taylor, *Leading an Evangelistic Youth Ministry* (Nashville: Lifeway, 1999), 14.
5. Ibid., 89.
6. Greg Stier, *Outbreak: Creating a Contagious Youth Ministry Through Viral Evangelism* (Chicago: Moody, 2002), 63.
7. Barna, *Real Teens,* 44.
8. George Barna, *Third Millennium* (Ventura, Calif.: Barna Research, 1999), 59.
9. Ross and Taylor, *Leading an Evangelistic Youth Ministry,* 17.
10. Douglas Hyde, *Rededication and Leadership* (South Bend, Ind.: University of Notre Dame Press, 1996), 17; cited in Stier, *Outbreak,* 58.
11. Stier, *Outbreak,* 195.

12. Ibid., 238.

Chapter 10: Every Move I Make

1. Greg Stier, *Outbreak: Creating a Contagious Youth Ministry Through Viral Evangelism* (Chicago: Moody, 2002), 81–82.
2. Ibid., 82.
3. George Barna, *Real Teens: A Contemporary Snapshot of Youth Culture* (Ventura, Calif.: Regal, 2001), 27.
4. Ibid.
5. Ibid., 31
6. Tim Stafford, "Has Christian Rock Lost Its Soul?" *Christianity Today,* 22 November 1993, 19.
7. Donald Hustad of Southern Seminary stated, "It should be obvious that the motivation behind all the pop-gospel phenomena of our day is evangelism." Donald Hustad, "Music in the Outreach of the Church" (Southern Baptist Church Music Conference, June 9–10, 1969), 48.
8. "Conn. 'Festival of Faith' Results in 120 Decisions," *Indiana Baptist,* 12 July 1972, 5.
9. Philip Landgrave, "Church Music and the 'Now Generation,'" *Review and Expositor* 69 (spring 1972): 195.
10. Forrest H. Heeren, "Church Music and Changing Worship Patterns," *Review and Expositor* 69 (spring 1972): 190.
11. John W. Styll, "Sound and Vision: Fifteen Years of Music and Ministry," *Contemporary Christian Music,* July 1993, 43.
12. "How to Get Signed in the '90s—Part 2," *Contemporary Christian Music,* July 1993, 24.
13. For more information on these and other more recent songs, go to www.worshiptogether.com.

Chapter 11: Advice to Parents

1. Victor Lee and Jerry Pipes, *Family to Family* (Atlanta: NAMB, 1999), 5.
2. Neil Howe and William Strauss, *Millennials Rising: The Next Great Generation* (New York: Vintage, 2000), 17.
3. Mark DeVries, "What Is Youth Ministry's Relationship to the Family?" in *Reaching a Generation for Christ,* eds. Richard R. Dunn and Mark H. Centers III (Chicago: Moody, 1997), 480.

4. Ibid., 489.

5. Lee and Pipes, *Family to Family,* 6.

6. Ibid.

7. Robert Lewis, *Raising a Modern-Day Knight* (Wheaton, Ill.: Tyndale House, 1997), 37–38.

8. Richard Ross and Len Taylor, *Leading an Evangelistic Youth Ministry* (Nashville: Lifeway, 1999), 22.

9. George Barna, *Real Teens: A Contemporary Snapshot of Youth Culture* (Ventura, Calif.: Regal, 2001), 68.

10. Ibid., 77.

11. Josh McDowell, *The Disconnected Generation* (Nashville: Word, 2000), 48, also 10.

12. Howe and Strauss, *Millennials Rising,* 17.

13. David Alan Black, *The Myth of Adolescence* (Yorba Linda, Calif.: Davidson, 1998), 21.

14. Barna, *Real Teens,* 54.

15. Ibid.

16. Dyan Machan in Howe and Strauss, *Millennials Rising,* 5.

17. Bess Keller, "Schools Seen as Out of Sync with Teens," 2 May 2001, http://www.magportal.com/cgi-bin/rdir.cgi?w=59642. Accessed 12 March 2002.

18. Richard R. Dunn, "Putting Youth Ministry into Perspective," in *Reaching a Generation for Christ,* eds. Richard R. Dunn and Mark H. Centers III (Chicago: Moody, 1997), 65.

19. Devries, "What Is Youth Ministry's Relationship to the Family?" 494.

20. Ben Patterson in DeVries, "What Is Youth Ministry's Relationship to the Family?" 493.

21. Barna, *Real Teens,* 57.

Chapter 12: Meanwhile, Back at the Church

1. George Barna, *Real Teens: A Contemporary Snapshot of Youth Culture* (Ventura, Calif.: Regal, 2001), 139.

2. Resources to help think through the big picture of youth ministry: Doug Fields, *Purpose-Driven Youth Ministry* (Grand Rapids: Zondervan, 1998); and Andy Stanley and Stuart Hall, *The Seven Checkpoints* (West Monroe, La.: Howard, 2001), who offer seven "checkpoints" on which to build youth ministry on either a two-year or four-year model.

3. The best discussion I have seen on this issue is the approach taken by Mark DeVries, "What Is Youth Ministry's Relationship to the Family?" in *Reaching a Generation for Christ*, eds. Richard R. Dunn and Mark H. Centers III (Chicago: Moody, 1997).

4. Further reading related to abolishing traditional youth ministry: (1) Hope Chapel, California: "Hope Chapel is committed to strengthening families, so it keeps them together as much as possible. This means that almost all home groups and Bible studies are geared for families and everyone of all ages. We do have some meetings just for men and just for ladies (adults 13 and up), as well as two annual adults-only banquets, but overall we try to keep families and singles together. This is obviously in contrast to the popular approach, which divides up families and intentionally segregates meetings and ministries by ages and marital status. Our specific goal is quite the opposite—to integrate all ages as much as possible" (from the web site www.hopechapel.cc). (2) Christopher Schlect, *Critique of Modern Youth Ministry* (Moscow, Idaho: Canon, 1995). (3) Mark Senter, ed., *Four Views of Youth Ministry* (Grand Rapids: Zondervan, 2001). (4) David Alan Black, *The Myth of Adolescence* (Yorba Linda, Calif.: Davidson, 1998).

5. Fields, *Purpose-Driven Youth Ministry*, 18.

6. Rick Warren, *The Purpose-Driven Church* (Grand Rapids: Zondervan, 1995).

7. Fields, *Purpose-Driven Youth Ministry*, 19–22.

8. Ibid., 39.

9. Stanley and Hall, *The Seven Checkpoints*, 8–9.

10. Ibid.

11. Frank Voight, "The Lifesaving Station," cited in John Kramp, *Out of Their Faces and into Their Shoes* (Nashville: Broadman and Holman, 1995).

Chapter 13: Rites of Passage

1. Robert Lewis, *Raising a Modern-Day Knight* (Wheaton, Ill.: Tyndale House, 1997), 10.

2. David Alan Black, *The Myth of Adolescence* (Yorba Linda, Calif.: Davidson, 1998), 60.

3. Richard N. Ostling and Joan K. Ostling, *Mormon America: The Power and the Promise* (San Francisco: Harper, 1999), 156–57.

4. Ibid., 51–59.